MW01120803

The Merrimack Literary Review

2004

EDITED BY

Ron Howland
&
Greg Waters

The Merrimack Literary Review

Andover, Massachusetts

THE MERRIMACK LITERARY REVIEW
Andover High School
Shawsheen Road
Andover, MA 01810

LitReview@comcast.net

Copyright © 2004

by The Merrimack Literary Review

DESIGNED BY JUSTIN HOWLAND

Manufactured in the United States of America

International Standard Serial Number
ISBN 0-9755604-0-9

JACKET ART: KATHLEEN DOYLE COOK

JACKET DESIGN: JAMES BATCHELDER

Love is no more possible than stars.

Preface

Culturally, artists are in the margins. Science and technology and business produce—products (duh), things you can buy and sell, stick in your pocket or bite or throw or shoot—things that matter.

Pun intended. Matter.

On this one, I honestly bow to pop singers: "We live in a material world." In our society, art, poetry, fiction are, at best, entertaining—thus profitable. In fact, we have a collective sneaking suspicion that "literature" is, profit aside, merely decorative, secondary, a vague pastime for academics, and where it really matters, pun intended, irrelevant.

Actually, I love true science and purposeful technology. Technology gives us lamplight and Novocain, pacemakers and coffeemakers. Science, true science, gives us vision. Microscopic and macroscopic. Microwave traces of the Big Bang. Red shift. A kaleidoscopic vision of swirling galaxies, of stars being born in a lightshow of violent majesty. And true science gives us insight. Quantum and cosmologic. Superstrings and black holes. Beautiful, really. Science also informs us—true science—of its limitations. In his Second Incompleteness Theorem, Kurt Gödel proved there are whole sets of mathematical truths that cannot be proved. Stated another way, the theorem seems to say that *rational thought can never penetrate to the final, the ultimate truth.* John Archibald Wheeler, physicist and Einstein biographer, put it this way: "There is nothing deader than an equation. Imagine that we take the carpet up in this room, and lay down on the floor a big sheet of paper and rule it off in one-foot squares. Then I get down and write in one square my best set of equations for the universe, and you get down and write yours, and we get the people we respect the most to write down their equation, till we have all the squares filled. We've worked our way to the door of the room. We wave our magic wand and give the command to those equations to put on wings and fly. Not one of them will fly. Yet there is some magic in this universe of ours, so that with the birds and the flowers and the trees and the sky, it flies!"

We forget that there are questions science and technology cannot answer. They are confined—by definition—to the empirical (material) world. Why do I exist? Why is there anything rather than nothing? What is good and not bad, moral versus not moral? Such a simple sounding question. Science could answer, for example—*what is the most efficient way to exterminate a people*? It could not answer if this is right or wrong. As a society we like to look for material answers. A chemical to make me better. A product. A thing. We're good at it. And that's our problem.

It reminds me of the old joke about the woman who stops at night to help a drunk searching frantically under a streetlight. It happens that the drunk has lost his keys while wandering in the woods. The woman asks, "Then why are you looking *here*?" And the drunk replies, "Because the light is better."

We laugh because the logic is both perfect and perfectly wrong. And we laugh because it is familiar. Too familiar. We recognize, a little embarrassedly, something of ourselves in any good joke.

I like to think the woman in the joke is a writer. Good chance, of course, the drunk is. Neither speculation gets me back to the point. And the point is this: there are some questions that are—like it or not—mystical matters. Non-material. What's good? What's beautiful? What's sacred? Why do I see—no—*how* do I see beauty, dignity, meaning at the moment I hold a dying child or parent or lover in my arms? Or more to the heart of the mystery, why do the Red Sox do it to us every year? Why does the smell of summer rain on pavement bring back to me the sweet-sad pang of lost youth? Of youth found? These are, indeed, mystical matters.

These are also why we have painters, poets, writers; why 14-year-old Jenny Feinberg's voice is as important in this book—and in my life and in yours—as important as the voice of the late Andre Dubus, whose "Letter to a Writers' Workshop" also appears in this review, capturing and humbling writers before setting them free to take their separate flights. It has to do with how Andre Dubus III's

House of Sand and Fog offers up a curse and a benediction, a microcosm of how we simultaneously fail and succeed in our collective humanity. How Gaby Uberto Beltre's prose poem, capturing the cool high stride of young love, is wed to Chath Piersath's haunting resurrection of his wounded, missing homeland. How when Rhina Espaillat stood in the White House, honored for her poetry, she stood for them—and us. It's how Peggy Rombach's watermelons breathe. It is how, as Annie Deppe writes, "the blindman's dog / wears a kind of a dog smile / as it nudges its master / back from the edge." It is how Greg Waters, grandson, sees across oceans, along a glassine thread of time, sees himself descending as his grandmother descends as a girl from a mountain in Europe. It is how love exists even though

> love is no more possible than stars,
> than the ache that stretches beyond the skin
> and is older than skin, no more possible
> than a universe leaping into time
> scented with berries and the quiverings
> of light in the sky of a summer night
> into which we have—somehow—been borne....

There are voices in this book that represent—arbitrarily perhaps, distinctly for certain—the Merrimack Valley in New England. And every other human incarnation. Young and old. Past and present. Lost and found. Future, too, according to my best guess. Whatever mistakes we as editors have made along the way, they are voices that matter.

Pun unintended and serendipitous.

These voices can save us, deliver us from ourselves. Deliver us to ourselves.

Ron Howland
June 2004

Foreword

My grandfather was a custodian at a junior high school. He would rescue old, discarded library books from the dumpster and adopt them. They would reside in our back shed and beckon to be taken down off the shelves and to be held open in order for their souls to be known and appreciated. This is where it began for me: in a shed, sitting on a bag of last autumn's leaves, reading tattered, orphaned books.

Now, when I visit home, I know I won't find my grandfather or the books. I won't even find the shed that housed them. What remains is the awe that began so many years ago, sparked by a man who knew that the value of a book didn't lie in a broken binding or a torn page. The value was in the lines of letters, the formation of thoughts and the ability of a wordsmith to transcend time and place. A book cannot be broken if it can be read. My grandfather taught me that.

I would like to think my love of writing grew out of my love of reading. I wanted to emulate the writers and poets that I read and to create stories and characters of my own. I find writing the toughest challenge I've ever attempted. That is why it will always be a part of my life. I only hope that a few of my attempts along the way will be worth my own critical eye. We'll see.

The Merrimack Literary Review has been another adventure for me in the realm of reading and writing. I appreciated books before, but to be a part of the selecting and editing of pieces, as well as the technical side of cover design and page layout, has only increased that appreciation.

The Merrimack Literary Review is a mix of old and new voices of all ages. Each page is an invitation for the reader to meet new people or to get reacquainted with old friends. The voices within will give you a good idea of the Merrimack Valley past, present and future.

My memories of reading take me back to the shed behind the house I shared with my grandfather as I was growing up. Books opened my eyes to the potential that writing has to offer. The voices included here support that realization. The awe that kept me turning pages, started me writing and led me to teaching English has been heightened even more by the writers you'll meet within these pages. From the youngest to the oldest, their voices blend to form a chorus of the Merrimack Valley that we should celebrate and be proud to call our own.

Greg Waters
June 2004

ACKNOWLEDGEMENTS

We wish to acknowledge, with great gratitude, James Conway, President & CEO of Courier Corporation, Andover resident and unsung friend of schools in Merrimack Valley. His support has been both material and visionary. When our confidence flagged, his quiet conviction did not. We never had the courage to tell him that when we went looking for a printer, we were just shooting for some shiny paper and some staples. A special thanks to Brett Linton, Courier Companies Manager of Digital Prepress, for his boundless energy and optimism, regardless of time of day—or night. We wish to acknowledge, with equal gratitude, Peter Anderson, principal of Andover High School. We strongly suspect that not only was this whole thing his idea, but he only pretended not to know what was involved in such a project. Peter believes in teachers and he especially believes in kids, reaching out to every one of them until each has a place in our school. If there is no place, he makes one.

Our thanks to Denise Doherty for her energy and acumen, and to Karen Kline, friend of the arts, who brought us to The Museum of Printing in North Andover, Massachusetts to meet with local artists, writers, teachers, printers and businesspeople; she sat us down and said, "So what are you going to create and how can these folks help?" Among the group we found Mark Schorr, poet, artist, Director of the Robert Frost Foundation, who guided us in a thousand ways. He connected us to author Paul Marion, co-editor of *The Bridge Review: Merrimack Valley Culture*, an online journal at the University of Massachusetts Lowell. Paul not only agreed to submit his own work, but also reached out to many of the authors included in this book. Thanks also to author Peggy Rambach, who teaches workshops throughout the Merrimack area; she was instrumental in tracking down, for submissions and permissions, talented young people in the Lawrence area.

Thank you to Ellen Howland and Karen Shaheen for advice, editing and a place to land; to our colleagues at Andover High School for doing their work—and ours—and to Justin Howland for flying in from Ji Lin Province in China and being asked to design a book before having a chance to eat or shower.

A special thank you to Kathy Zalla, teacher and friend, who edited, typed, re-edited, re-typed, advised, and shaped up this book (and its editors). *She* knows an Oxford comma when she sees it. She also knows what is true and beautiful in language—and what is not. She knows that the secret to life is this: work hard on something that matters, and when it is done, no matter the result, laugh. KZ has, in fact, the most distinctive laugh that ever rose from the Merrimack Valley.

Finally, thanks to Andre Dubus III, for doing so much for us and for this book. He made us promise not to say all that he does for young and disenfranchised voices. We're only half-keeping that promise. In return, let the record show, we bought him only one cup of coffee.

But it was good coffee.

CONTENTS

CONTENTS

CONTENTS

CONTENTS

CONTENTS

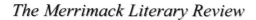

Telling stories and hearing them and reading them
is what joins us to one another.

Andre Dubus III

INTRODUCTION

I've lived in the Merrimack Valley most of my life, though I have not always enjoyed my time here: in the past, I associated it with my parents' divorce, the poverty that followed, the violence I witnessed and was part of. In 1969 we lived in Merrimac Port on a tree-lined street two blocks from the river. I had a friend whose family owned a brick house on the water, and his older brother was a soldier in Vietnam. When he got hurt, he was given something called a Purple Heart, and somehow, in my nine year old thinking, I came to believe that's why my parents separated too because they had Purple Hearts.

In 1970 my mother, brother, sisters, and I ended up in Newburyport, which was an abandoned collection of mill buildings where the Merrimack River gushes into the Atlantic. Downtown was deserted: the three-story brick buildings along State Street had no glass where their windows used to be, just gaping holes into dusty, empty rooms. Market Square was overgrown with waist-high weeds. Wrecked cars rusted themselves out on side streets. And we lived in three different houses on the south side where more than once drunks would walk into the house from the cracked sidewalk, my big sister chasing them out with a broom handle. I was small, and until a few years later when I began to fight back, I got beat up a lot. Two of the boys I feared the most are gone now, one dead, the other in prison for life.

In the early seventies we moved to Haverhill. First we lived in a one-story rental that used to be a doctor's office. The two years we were there, perfectly nice people would open our front door, sit in our cluttered living room and look around for something to read. We kids would be there on the floor, watching TV. It was a little scary but fun to look over and say the doctor had moved. We lived in other houses, finally settling into a big Victorian off Main Street that my mother could barely afford, even with Pop's child support. Still it had enough bedrooms for us all, a small back yard with grass, and neighbors who seemed nice enough, though they didn't like my brother's and my long hair, the young men on motorcycles my sister attracted.

We lived here for six years. It was a street of clean, well-maintained houses, but my brother, older sister, and I spent too much time on the other side of Main, down in the avenues in welfare apartments where there were always loud parties and Hells Angels, where there were tough girls in tight hip-huggers and tube tops, smoking Kools and acting cooler.

I started taking better care of myself; I began to lift weights, box, and run. I used to train at a gym in the factory district two blocks from the river. In the summer the windows would be open, and as I threw combinations at the light bag then the medium then the heavy, as I shadow-boxed in the ring, then sparred with whoever was there—Smiling Ray, who was handsome and always smiling, even when he had to go back to Walpole; Joey M., who years later became a male stripper down in Florida; Tony C., whose old man sold brass knuckles, boot knives, and saps to cops. I could smell the Merrimack—the raw sewage and tanning dye, the spilled fuel and dead fish and muddy banks littered with trash. And it occurred to me then that it wasn't a bad smell, simply one I knew so well, one that smelled like home to me, really.

Home.

At nineteen, I went to college in Texas then roamed the country for ten years, writing and working odd jobs, but always I came back to the Valley: to Haverhill to visit friends and my father; to Newburyport where I met my wife and had our three children; to Amesbury where my mother, brother, and sisters live; to Lowell where I now teach writing to wonderful students, many of whom have lived childhoods far rougher than mine ever was, many of whom have begun to write the stories only they can write. They come from Irish families, Cambodian, French Canadian, Polish, Latino, Greek, Jewish, Haitian, Vietnamese, Indian, and Filipino; and they already instinctively know what the writers in this volume know—from Jack Kerouac and my late father, Andre Dubus, to all these gifted high school students who are just beginning to find their voice and their subject—that telling stories and hearing them and reading them is what joins us to one another; it's what heals old wounds and captures new joys; it's what illuminates trouble and hope up ahead.

The editors here, Ron Howland and Greg Waters, know this. They know the inherent beauty and richness of this place, and this volume is a celebration of that: the Merrimack Valley and its people, their river of stories that can sweep us up and carry us off and, ultimately, save us.

Andre Dubus III
Newburyport, Massachusetts

what are you searching for
circling
      night in   *and*
      day out?

          ~Athena Hsieh

Robert Frost

MENDING WALL

Something there is that doesn't love a wall,
That sends the frozen-ground-swell under it,
And spills the upper boulders in the sun;
And makes gaps even two can pass abreast.
The work of hunters is another thing:
I have come after them and made repair
Where they have left not one stone on a stone,
But they would have the rabbit out of hiding,
To please the yelping dogs. The gaps I mean,
No one has seen them made or heard them made,
But at spring mending-time we find them there.
I let my neighbour know beyond the hill;
And on a day we meet to walk the line
And set the wall between us once again.
We keep the wall between us as we go.
To each the boulders that have fallen to each.
And some are loaves and some so nearly balls
We have to use a spell to make them balance:
"Stay where you are until our backs are turned!"
We wear our fingers rough with handling them.
Oh, just another kind of out-door game,
One on a side. It comes to little more:
There where it is we do not need the wall:
He is all pine and I am apple orchard.

My apple trees will never get across
And eat the cones under his pines, I tell him.
He only says, "Good fences make good neighbours."
Spring is the mischief in me, and I wonder
If I could put a notion in his head:
"Why do they make good neighbours? Isn't it
Where there are cows? But here there are no cows.
Before I built a wall I'd ask to know
What I was walling in or walling out,
And to whom I was like to give offence.
Something there is that doesn't love a wall,
That wants it down." I could say "Elves" to him,
But it's not elves exactly, and I'd rather
He said it for himself. I see him there
Bringing a stone grasped firmly by the top
In each hand, like an old-stone savage armed.
He moves in darkness as it seems to me,
Not of woods only and the shade of trees.
He will not go behind his father's saying,
And he likes having thought of it so well
He says again, "Good fences make good neighbours."

From North of Boston, *1915*

9

Athena Hsieh

TWO POEMS

1.

little man
with your big, sad face
and soulless eyes.
what are you searching for?
circling
    night in   and
    day out.
chasing your bright counterpart
who lights up your eyes.
but don't run away from me.
you light up my night
and take happiness with you
as the new day rises
and the waning dark fades.
i see you –
    i see you not.

but come the next black,
    velvety night,
    i shall await you
as you continue your search,
circling
ever on
and on.

2.

beach.
sandy night.
lift me into the air
and fly me away from here.
take me home beneath the crashing waves.
let me taste the salty water in my lungs
and feel it in my heart.

and then
i'll exhale —

Jack Kerouac

GO BACK

One night I sat on the curbstone of a street in the city and looked across the road at a little rose-covered cottage which was rickety, like the fence around it, and it looked old, not Colonial, but old. That's where I used to live, I said aloud to myself in a tone of yearning. I tried to sigh like they do in plays, but it was a fake one. I didn't want to sigh, but I tried. The thing I really wanted to do was weep, but I couldn't do that either.

The city was all about me, and the electric lamp above me, and the house was there and my memories flashed through my head and the scene before me supplemented them. I, small and dreamy, dashing about—over the banister, up that old tree of mine, around the yard, through the back fences......and the shed with the old organ in it, and the sounds I used to hear and now they are dissolved, their scientific sound waves far away.

I saw a man walking toward his destination and I felt bad. He was hurrying, and I was sitting thinking about the past. The dream I used to have......snow, tinkling icicles, laughter, sunshine, sleighs......and the nightmares too. And the man was hurrying and I was sitting quietly, staring at my old home.

The old cat, I thought, a bundle of bones now, somewhere. The cat who used to sit right there on the porch, placidly enjoying his digestion.

Later on, I left and I went toward the house before that, where my brother had died. Here, the memories were now vague and childish. I was three and four there, three and four years old.

I remember the high snow, my sandwich, calling for my mother, weeping, all. Myself.....at the church.....unabashed, they burying my brother. Why do you cry, I ask my mother and sister. Why do you cry? Why?

Now a man comes up the street and walks right into my old house.

Zounds, I say. Zounds! You hurry while I stand here, trying to recapture the past. And here you are, brushing it aside, the past of tomorrow, which is the present of today, you are brushing it aside as you stride along, intent on your cheap present practical and physical desires and comfort. You fool! Wait, don't hurry.

Get out of my old house!

And then on the way home, I think about the fool and the other fools, and myself a fool. Hurrying away the past of tomorrow, like I had hurried away the past of today, in the past.

Fools, I think. Myself a fool. I must take it slow now and look at the present and say to myself: Look, John, hold the present now because someday it will be very precious. Hug it, and hold it.

And just yesterday I was sauntering home thinking about the future. The future! What a fool, I , myself, a fool, hurrying.

Summer 1940

Nancy Meyers

PRESSURE

overloads, explodes

transformed into heat that radiates

molded and structured into someone, someone else

every imperfection, every mistake magnified

depicted and discussed

Ron Howland

UNDER TEN

~*1*~

Cameroon had taken the field under a pink sky. One by one the players were virtually lifted by their shoulders and placed into position. Usually they fidgeted and danced in a circle of hands. Usually you heard the word *silly*. You heard patience in adult voices. Good humor. You heard the names of children. But they were subdued that early evening prior to the whistle that would never come to start the game. Everyone was quiet, as if stilled by the colors of the evening As if it were better not to move across the world because the colors were still wet.

The hands of the coaches were gentle, their reassuring voices whispery across the August grass. Soundless words blew out like damp matches on the field, drifted past parents in lawn chairs at the edge of a chalk boundary, drifted across Camrys and Volvos and Tauruses. East toward the sea. Toward the darker sky. Night.

Above the green-brown field, time hung pink. Corintha watched her son. She adored his legs, tan as a dove in morning light. His hands in this strange and perfect light glowed like the hands of ancient children, like hands painted in a cave. His shirt—the shirts of all the children representing suburban Cameroon—were the softest green, like cream in a Key lime pie. Corintha said, "They look like desserts." She spoke to no one. No one heard. It was like mouthing strange words in an unfamiliar chapel. And she smiled.

Corintha's son looked with green-brown eyes straight up into the sky, down along the treetops, down through transparent people seated on lawn chairs and into the ragged blackness beyond the further edge of the parking lot where the weeds

15

turned infinite and wild. Corintha heard a woman call out, "Be aggressive, Michelle. Don't back away from the ball." Her voice was shy and embarrassed, followed by the reassuring voices of fathers teasing her. Corintha thought, *Be aggressive, Nathaniel,* like a rote prayer that needn't be answered. He was fine as he was. He looked like a dessert. The woman's name was Jennings. Mrs. Jennings with no first name had now stood up in mock indignation. Her bottom was wide and saggy like a rack of discontinued canvas bags. She was so human you wanted to cry.

Corintha looked out again across the field as her son Nathaniel, an Under 10, reversed the path of his vision. The weeds, the tree tops, the sky. She watched him seeing. Corintha's eyes fluttered like eyes in rain. It was as if a twig were snapping in the weeds behind her, and she was almost standing over him as he lay on the field with his legs half crossed like a hastily written four. Nathaniel had worn the number three for suburban Cameroon. The uniforms had all come through with the number three. That had been the joke of the summer. "Which one is yours?" someone would ask. You would say, "Number three," pointing outward onto the field beyond the chalk boundary at your feet. "Number three," as if, with good-natured irony, that were enough. As if that explained everything.

For Corintha neither the funeral nor the condolences were enough just as their finding the frightened, deficient older boy in the weeds had explained nothing. Roger. Startled Roger for whom everyone had always applauded politely at school functions. Had always called "nice try" the year he tried instructional Little League although he was two years too old, too preposterously passive and too big. Special Roger whom they removed from class from time to time for Special Help. He had been found without any effort, squatting in the weeds, shocked even more than competent adults that he could have hit anything with such accuracy from such a distance. That it took so long for someone to come.

Roger understood just enough to know that it was more chance than anything that the bullet struck what he had aimed at. He had been copying something from the news:

A playground shooting in the city. A microphone man on TV. When he heard Nathaniel talking about it at school, he told a court officer, it was "sorta Nate told me to do it."

Did he mean to kill him? No, he didn't mean to. He meant only to shoot. Later he told a judge that "it wasn't real." The lie was uncharacteristic. Roger was not too simple to lie, he had never been given a reason to. He was encouraged and forgiven in everything. That was before Nathaniel died. It all became real in that moment. It was even real to Roger. Especially real.

From the state Roger received a Special Placement which, after all, was right. Even Corintha knew it was right because it didn't much matter.

After a time, in the evenings, she began to have waking dreams, which altered the images of the day. She looked on at the edge of her wet-color dreams. So did Jay Silverheels. He was handsome and only a little ironic, an attitude that made his sincerity and the visions themselves more real. She told her husband, Mark, who was alarmed enough to suggest that they get help. By *they* he meant Corintha.

Corintha ended her grief counseling during the third visit. She had failed to tap the anger and denial and the guilt she did not feel. She had been told at the outset by Jeannie with the gypsy hoops in her ears that it was uncharacteristic of a woman to feel a need to impose rational understandings on the events of their lives, which Corintha took to mean reasons. And reasons, she was told, was what she was looking for.

Corintha said, No, she didn't think so. She wanted the meaning of things. Jeannie had always used the word *things* when she meant Nathaniel's death. And Jeannie was wrong: the men Corintha knew didn't piece out the reason for things any more than women did. They simply occupied themselves, like any developed people, with the familiar.

Corintha understood her therapy completely. Jeannie believed in the unresolved conflict of universal grief: denial, anger, guilt, fear. Procedurally and necessarily these must come before sadness and acceptance. But Corintha already accepted her sadness. That wasn't it. She believed in her experience completely. She had experienced her boy's death. Now she experienced waking dreams.

Without divulging the presence of Tonto, Corintha told her most recent dream to Jeannie. While driving to the bank earlier in the day, Corintha had seen older boys playing basketball on a paved lot near the center of town. They were vulgar and rough with one another and frequently slipped, trying to change directions in their heavy black boots. They were in jeans, shirtless, and their hair was long. That night when she sat in the yard in the last light of the day, she saw them more clearly playing in front of her. She could hear the sand scuff beneath their boosts, see the perspiration on their chests, the blemishes, the hair wild and infinite against green plains that swept beyond them to the west, and against the permanent crescent of ice on the northern horizon. Above it all and to the east, night. A part of her leaned out of herself, yearning, almost sexually.

The requisite Freudian pause.

"And how are you and Mark?" Jeannie asked.

"Are you by any chance Indian?" Corintha asked.

"No. Do you mean Native? No."

"Mexican?"

"No." She looked at the silver rings on her aging hands, thinking young crone. She smiled appreciatively at her own hands. "No, but I love Mexican things."

-2-

To the southwest, along the horizons of her visions, Corintha could see the rim of the Mexican desert blowing its rose talc over the thin membrane of planetary air. Closer by she could have seen blurred little cities, like blue carcinomas embedded in the skin of the continent, but she preferred the rose beauty of Mexican distance. We know, because of this, that her waking dreams, for want of better words, were not delusions and not supernatural visitations. Because of choice, that is. Corintha chose, as much as any of us chooses, what fraction she would look at in all that appeared before her.

She was one of those people—and there are really only three kinds—who like distances. We can pretend that cosmologists, goatherds, poets, archaeologists, fighter pilots, pacifists, preachers and assassins are different, but they are all enchanted by panoramas. Just as surgeons, onanists and stamp collectors are drawn to miniature detail.

Corintha was one who looked outward. She looked northward to the darkening polar cap and saw auroras arcing faintly green, leaving the earth altogether. She had quit close things. She believed, inaccurately, that she could quit everything close. Her therapy and her work at the bank. Her marriage. Weeds.

After nearly a month passed, she began to see at the edge of her waking dreams, where the timeless flux of earthly distance spilled onto her suburban lawn, not Jay Silverheels but Mr. McPherson, her tenth grade English teacher. Unlike Silverheels he stood without irony. Like Silverheels he stood without trembling hands, never watching Corintha, although aware of her, but watching instead the figures of her visions. In life, whatever life there can be said to be in the tenth grade, Mr. McPherson's hands had trembled. The midpoint of his upper lip came to a point when he spoke—moist, deliberate and vulnerable like the anterior of a worm. The moment it exposed itself it drew back. Perhaps it was more like the underside of a snail. Corintha had done well in sophomore biology.

Behind his back, the students had called him Mr. McQueerson. They imitated his tremulous hands. In class they ridiculed him with subtle deception, asking him to recite the poems they were studying in class and flexing their lips in silent unison as he read. Corintha never derided Mr. McPherson, but like her classmates she didn't like poetry. She would simply occupy herself by looking at the tentative moisture of a lip and hearing, where she might have listened for meanings, the sad and lonely sound of barely audible beauty.

One day, after having appeared for several weeks in the margins of her visions, he appeared both as the observer from the edges and as a figure at the center of a dream. A classmate named Brian—it was happening almost exactly as it had happened twenty years before—is craning his head around impatiently, disgusted with the eternal monotony of literature. He is saying, just as he had said a fifth of a century earlier, "Jesus, Mr. McPherson"—he has the voice of a redhead—"is all they ever write about love and death?" Without looking up, Mr. McPherson says, "What else is there." It isn't a question.

After that exchange neither McPherson nor Silverheels appeared along the chalky boundary of her dreams. The visions still occurred, but Corintha stood up and walked away from them, restless and distracted with the feeling that something was missing. There was no one else with her. No spectator looking on as she looked on. She called a former classmate who told her that five years before—I think that's right, yes five, said the voice that had long ago lost its face—Mr. McPherson died of AIDS. That rumor was not true. He contracted AIDS. He died of sorrow.

For nearly a month in September, just as the current school year started, Mr. McPherson had appeared at the edges of her visions. Then one day he disappeared. What else is there? It was the last thing he said. It wasn't a question. He was so human you wanted to cry.

In the last week of September, Corintha called and left a message for "someone who loved the teaching of poetry" to please call with a suggested selection—"something that is about love and death and feels like a waking dream." They passed that one around the English Department like a bad joke. Receiving no return call, Corintha wrote a note to the high school repeating her request. The letter arrived on the first day of October. Three days before the new moon. Although Corintha did not know the name, she had described Katherine Jeffers in her note with such peculiar accuracy that young Mrs. Jeffers felt compelled to write back. Anyone could have known that she had "chestnut skin and is rather pretty, except for short hair like a boy." After all, she taught in a public school. But who would have known that, on the last night of September, the night before Corintha's letter arrived at school, Katherine wore "earrings like impossibly long drops of gold." That evening Katherine's new husband had just given his wife the lovely and unusual pendant rings to mark a lovely and unusual intimacy between the new couple.

Intrigued and wary, even a little frightened, Katherine wrote a short, cool letter to "the nut lady," as the Department had referred to her, including with the note a photocopy of a poem called "Crossings" by Linda Hogan. "Have we met?" Katherine's note began. "If so, I do not recall...."

No reply. No 'thank you.' Mrs. Jeffers might have left their two lives at a near miss if it weren't for the specter of earrings that grew beyond the intimacy of their origin. Katherine even grilled her innocent husband about their purchase, but he had bought them in the city, paid cash and divulged nothing in his conversation to the sales representative, a man, except to say "Wow, those are unusual." It was an upscale shop where one rarely said wow. On the third day of Catherine's sweet interrogations, her husband broke down and admitted, in fact, to having said *wow*. He refused to further wrack his memory for something he could not recall. And he suggested that Catherine forget the whole thing, or ask someone at work if they had ever heard of Corintha, or contact the woman directly.

When Katherine heard that her eerie correspondent was the woman whose son was killed in the summer, not only did her suspicions evaporate—she felt fear, of course, but it is the natural fear you have for your unborn—and not only did she feel sorrow, she felt a compelling need to do something. It was an emotion beyond empathy. It was something approaching love.

And so they met.

Katherine was becoming accustomed to standing twice a week at the edge of Corintha's lawn and seeing Corintha seated at the periphery of her own vision which saw nothing but the last light of day fading out of the suburbs of the Americas. It was enough that Corintha saw. When night came they would talk. Corintha at first apologized that she could not see Africa, assuming graciously and foolishly that this would be something gratifying to Katherine. If Corintha tried to look back to the east, to the lands of either woman's origins, she saw only night. Africa appeared only as a thin line on the horizon. It looked blue and surprisingly cool.

The nights turned cool. Night came earlier and earlier, and Katherine waited, knowing with sadness and with hope that every story has an ending. One night three days beyond the quarter moon that could not be seen in a cloudless sky, Katherine stood while Corintha remained seated and motionless long after the last glow of day, the time when she had always before finished her waking dreams. Katherine did not want to interrupt but it was getting late. She was cold and pleasantly drowsy. Drifting. She had begun picturing her young husband. She could feel his starchy collar on her neck. His fragrance. The smell of wood smoke. Fallen leaves. The smell of green wood broken in a May squall. The wetness of birth. Corintha was not in her chair.

The shrubs at the corner of the foundation rustled. It was a windless night across which Katherine did not move and could barely see. She looked with green-brown eyes straight up into the sky, down along the treetops, past the chalk boundary of her educated mind and into the ragged blackness beyond the further edge of the lawn here the weeds turned infinite and wild. "Corintha?" she said.

Yes. Katherine did not exactly hear Corintha's answer. She felt it. She saw Corintha's figure at the far end of the yard near black weeds grown taller than a human. Wild and infinite and swayed by invisible winds. Pale, almost imperceptible shadows seeped from beneath the weeds. Green shadows. Pink.

No, Katherine said. She called out with her mind. *No. Don't.* Her eyes fluttered like eyes in the rain.

No? Corintha's unspoken voice carried the tone of our mothers when we are very young. The soft irony of our first teachers. Katherine heard the voice in her thoughts saying softly and stubbornly, *Yes.*

There is a meaning to every story. A moral. A good deal of our literature for a good while now insists there is not. The best writing frequently contradicts its own beauty and is acclaimed for its ambiguous effects. Whether it is a cause or a result, we are a people who prefer newspapers. We watch microphone people on television speaking from the margins, their backs turned to the people they should be facing.

The moral of Corintha's story is simple. We enter this life and witness a world where visions appear and disappear. People appear and disappear. We disappear.

Jason Edelstein

ANDOVER, LAWRENCE, AND ITALY

I remember receiving a formal introduction to geography when I was a student in middle school. My colleagues and I were exposed to the world and its variety of cultures from the comfort of an Andover West Middle School classroom. For some, the idea of learning geography seemed trivial because it wasn't directly applicable to the real world model that parents were concerned with. But unlike some of my peers, I was embarrassed by how lost I was within my contained world.

There was one particular activity from sixth grade that opened my eyes to the possibility that I could make sense of what was around me. My history teacher had suggested to our class that we try to fill out a blank map. So innocent, I remember exuding a smiley confidence since I had memorized all fifty of the United States as an elementary school student. A simple task like filling in a map wouldn't pose a threat.

A stack of stock, eight-and-a-half-by-eleven paper was passed down the rows of desks, one to each student. When I placed my hands on the sheet and turned it over, I was a bit confused. The map sitting before me didn't have the recognizable curves of the United States, or North America. Instead it was something very different. Something that didn't sink in for a while. There was an initial panic being stirred within my system, fueled by a shot of adrenaline. I was more concerned by the grade I would receive on such an assignment and not by what kind of enlightenment I could gain from what was on that paper.

The teacher hinted to us that what we were looking at was a map of suburban towns and cities along the northeastern coast of Massachusetts. The places that I crossed into, after leaving the outer limits of my hometown, were represented by their proper boundary lines. Our job, as I remember being instructed, was to simply fill in the names of the particular places represented by the map.

The second hand raced around the clock several times before I had even begun to fill the map in. I tried to think about places my mom had taken me to do errands. I tried to think of the beaches I had been to and the towns they were located in. But I really wasn't sure where they belonged on the map. In fact, I didn't really know where any of the towns fit on the map. I started to realize that in all my years of schooling, I had failed to locate myself.

I'm not sure how much time passed before the identities of the places were revealed. I'd been distracted, daydreaming about places I'd been and the things I thought characterized those places. Several of the towns and cities adjacent to Andover were pointed out to us. I had a few of these place names written down on my map, but I didn't remember that Lowell was to the west of Andover. I just think of the historic canals and mills when I think of Lowell. It's like Andover, only bigger and more urban, so it's a city, not a town. It turns out that Tewksbury is to the south of Andover. I had it on my map, but not in the right spot. I could never really think of a distinction between Andover and Tewksbury, other than the difference between their superior high school football team and our lackluster one. When the teacher mentioned Lawrence, I was surprised that I had forgotten it. I never really thought much of Lawrence, at least at that time anyway. It stands in contrast to Andover as an inner city school would a suburban prep school. Though Andover and Lawrence are adjacent to each other, the only things I could think of that they had in common were Route 28 and the Merrimack River. And there were many towns sharing those two things.

When I scanned the map again, I didn't notice any indications of disparity in income between Andover and its neighbor to the north, Lawrence. The curriculum at our school was based mostly on far off places, and about people I would never meet. I didn't understand why I had never studied all the culture of a city so close to my own home. It was as though Lawrence had been hidden from me.

*   *   *

During my junior year of high school I had applied and was hired to work in a local restaurant called Bertucci's. I was familiar with the restaurant, which served traditional Italian dishes and specialized in brick oven pizza. Ironically, Bertucci's authentic Italian cuisine was prepared by a cooking staff made up of young Hispanic men and women from Lawrence. To fill out the staff, the managers of the restaurant employed residents of Andover, like myself, to man the front of the house and serve the tables. Although I was initially concerned about how such a rift would affect a staff, the distinction between the two groups of workers seemed minimal. In fact, I enjoyed the harmony in which we all worked. It really wasn't until I became brotherly with some of the cooks that I noticed how much more their lives were challenged than my own. At the end of the night, when we went to the parking lot to leave for our homes, things weren't as homogenous as one might have expected. Although we shared the responsibility inside the work place, we lived very separate lives outside. The cars we drove weren't the same, and certainly the homes we were headed to were anything but similar.

As I spent more time working at the restaurant, I noticed myself spending more time in the kitchen. I'd hear the sound of my name disappear into the air just as I'd walk by the cooks. They were all native Spanish speakers. When I talked with them, I asked questions, and they were always open to sharing their feelings. Most of my coworkers had emigrated from the Dominican or Brazil. I remember at first struggling to understand all the things coming out of their mouths. Some of the Spanish started to sit better on my tongue. My accent progressed far more at work than it did in the classroom. I still wanted to know more about them; I just didn't know enough about them to ask the right question.

After a few months, the cultures surrounding me pieced themselves together. The cooks started calling me *Peluca* because none of the guys in Lawrence had locks as long as mine. The cooks just hadn't seen any guys in Lawrence walking around with long shaggy hair. The way my hair flipped upwards around my ears reminded them of the way Halle Berry styles hers. One of my coworkers even thought I was wearing a wig, and that's where my nickname came from.

I've enjoyed my time at the restaurant and learned all kinds of significant things from them. It would often start with something simple like how to chop basil properly. I'd always work slowly because we'd start talking about something else, like how their family values were so much stronger than those of the Americans around them. I learned about so many things not mentioned in the classroom, but that were, nevertheless, imperative to me if I ever hoped to become cultured.

After a while, I got close to the little family the cooks had formed, and I felt sympathetic toward the hardships they faced. Never before had I seen such stoicism. I was afraid they'd be fated to work forty-plus-hour weeks forever, concerned they were not able to go to a proper school because they would have to stop working, something they couldn't do. I felt ashamed for living so luxuriously all my life and not appreciating it.

*   *   *

Gerson taught me the most. He knew just enough English to change my life and many of my values. I'd work side by side with him for months, piecing his story together, learning a little more about him each shift. I'd glean some information from the other employees, pick up on things he said. I knew he lived in Lawrence, and after a few months I knew he had brothers and sisters, and I knew he was the best person I'd ever meet.

He was only two years older than I, nineteen at the time, but he was some ten years more mature than I was. He went to college. He worked full time. He lived a tough life and never complained. It wasn't that he was hiding his true feelings; he just had the best attitude of anyone I'd ever come in contact with. We'd talk about going to the gym. I'd just started going before school. He told me he did the same; it was the only extra time he had. He used to say, "I want to lift three plates today, each side. I just want to feel it; I'm going to do it. Oh, man, I just can't wait—in five years I'll be huge." That was enough inspiration for me. How could I ever say that I was too tired to get up and get to the gym? How could I ever say I was too tired to do anything?

Gerson worked for a different reason than I did. He told me, "This ain't living—working to help pay rent. This isn't it." It took me a little while to piece what he said together. I realized that he was helping to support his family. I guess I'd just never heard anyone having to do something like that for his or her family.

After six months of work, I'd become closer to the cooks than the hosts and wait staff members I worked beside. They were my friends, sometimes my adversaries. A year has now passed, and I'm still working side by side with Gerson. Some of the cooks have left, found other jobs. One is going to be a policeman. It seems that maybe all their hard work is going to pay off. Gerson once mentioned he wanted to go to Harvard. He said he wanted to learn about computers. I think he'd do well there, and it upsets me that he's denied the opportunity I have. I feel lucky to have gotten a wake up call. More than ever I want to make something of myself. I want to capitalize on what's been set before me. Now when I drift off at work, I think about giving back. I think about becoming successful and making a difference. I dream of helping people. As I look back now, I smile at the fact that I thought I was working.

Rachel Knox Alesse

SHELLFISH

He drives us back to the funeral home, and we walk up to the double oak doors and push through them. The dark green carpet of the foyer muffles our footsteps. Hallways jut to the left and right. Straight ahead, the main room lies beyond propped open doors, guarded by potted ferns on pedestals. Uncle Troy and I go in, our every movement dying quickly in the breathless air. Fifty-some odd eyes are watching me. I sit next to Bug and take her hand. A man, the Funeral Director I suppose, walks in from a door in the back. As he passes a window I notice that in the heat, a tree outside has dropped all but a few of its flowers. The man walks in front of Mom's casket, which is closed. He rearranges some papers at the podium and clears his throat.

"Jen," Bug whispers, "fish scales look like this."

I can't take my eyes off the casket. How sturdy and polished it is, like a dinner table. The gold handles on the sides could be drawer pulls for all their gilded efficiency. For the first time today it strikes me how wrong all this is. There's a piece of furniture where my mom should be.

Bug is pulling on my sleeve, pointing at the black sequins on a woman's hat. Fish scales. She looks at Aunt Lily and pats her arm. I feel the gleam of Uncle Troy's eye slide over me.

"And Jen," Bug clutches my arm now, "Mom is here! Aunt Lily said! She *is*!"

Bug is bouncing in her chair. She bares her teeth and squints her eyes into flat slits. She thumps her red-glowing cheek with the back of her hand. "Mommy's here!" she cries.

Someone starts sobbing in the seats behind us.

"No Beatrice," Aunt Lily cautions, "your mother is—"

"Mommy!" she cries, "I want Mommy!"

"No Beatrice!" Aunt Lily says shakily.

Uncle Troy looks to the man standing beside my mother's casket and checks his watch.

I told Bug about the funeral this morning.

"The *funeral*," I explained, "will be quiet. Lots of people that we know will be there. Mom will be there. You will see her, but she will be *dead*. She won't hear or see you. Everyone will be sad. They will tell us they are sorry that Mom is *dead*."

Bug had smiled too hard.

"Bug," I said, "after the funeral we won't see Mom anymore. She'll be gone."

"When is she coming back?" Bug had asked.

"She's not."

Bug had taken that in, squinting and grimacing while she thumped her cheek with the back of her hand. I tied her shoes. It was going to be a long walk to Mom's funeral.

The pantyhose and cheap shoes were a bad mix. After two blocks my feet were stinging hot. The dress I bought was too heavy for the relentless explosion of heat that pressed against us. Bug was moving along slowly, humming and watching her shoelaces. I stopped every few yards to make sure she didn't hit anything, bent over as she was, lurching left to right down the sidewalk. We were late.

It wasn't the distance that bogged us down; the funeral home was just a mile away. It was the heat and pressure of the day and the weird sense of being pushed back.

We had nearly made it when I heard a car slow down and its tires scratch to a gritty stop beside us. I knew who was there, but I kept us walking until I heard my name shoved at me.

Uncle Troy was hanging off the steering wheel glaring at me through the open window. Aunt Lily was in the back looking crushed under the diagonal band of her seat belt.

My feet hurt so badly I didn't resist. I opened the rear door for Bug.

"Hi Beatrice!" Aunt Lily said brightly, although she flinched as

Bug stumbled into the seat.

"I've been calling you for days, why didn't you wait for us, why are you walking?" As he yelled, I could see where Uncle Troy's teeth ended at the back of his mouth, and where the gray delta of enamel flowed along his tooth beds.

I rolled my eyes as I slid into the passenger seat.

"And what's with the hair?"

"You don't like it?"

Uncle Troy shook his head in disbelief and glared at the road. "I should have expected this from you," he said.

"We were walking because Mom's car was totaled," I said.

"We're going to a *few*-ner-all," Bug added. I wanted to reach between the seats and high-five her.

Uncle Troy's lips went hard until he pulled into the circular drive in front of Lake's Funeral Home. He put the car in "park" and swiveled to face the back seat.

"Lily, take Beatrice in," he said sharply.

Bug and Aunt Lily looked at each other apprehensively. He took a deep breath and turned back around. He let the air out of his lungs slowly and started rubbing the steering wheel with both hands.

"Hey, Beatrice," he finally said to Bug via the rearview mirror, "Why don't lobsters share?"

Bug recognizes a joke when she hears one. She drew her chubby knees together and rubbed her chin with the back of her hand.

"Don't know!" she finally admitted.

Uncle Troy turned around and smiled at her. "Because they're shellfish!"

"Shellfish!" She echoed, but she didn't get it. Bug has no idea what it is to be selfish, and she's never seen so much as a clam. Her clear brown eyes narrowed as she thought it over. "Fish have shells," she decided.

"No, no they don't—" Uncle Troy stammered, turning to catch Bug's eye. "No, Beatrice, fish have *scales*."

Bug's face brightened. "I have snails in my grass!" She

clapped and rubbed her chin.

"You're only going to confuse her," I muttered.

"Confuse her? More than she is now? That's just the trouble with you and—" he stalled "—and your mother. Coddling her. It's unconscionable. She needs to get out and learn about the world."

Before I could say anything, he thrust his chin at the roof of the car. "Fish have *scales*, Beatrice," he announced. "Some fish, called mollusks, live in *shells*."

"A lobster isn't a mollusk; it's a crustacean, you moron," I snorted.

"Troy," Aunt Lily piped up, "let's not get in to this now."

"Just take her," he snapped.

At first nobody moved. I gave Uncle Troy a long look. I stretched it out like gum, twirling it shamelessly around my finger. Finally I cleared my throat and said "Bug, Aunt Lily is going to take you inside to see some flowers."

"Oh good!" Bug tugged on Aunt Lily's blazer as Aunt Lily fumbled with her seat belt.

Uncle Troy drove without speaking. His hands squeezed the steering wheel. He parked under a tree not far from Lake's and just sat there. Sensing that we were in limbo, my feet started to throb. Something fell out of the tree, a nut by its sharp sound, and hit the roof of the car. Uncle Troy took that as his cue.

"Jen, as I mentioned, I have been trying to reach you. We have to talk about unpleasant things."

"Really."

"Your mother loved you and Beatrice very much."

"You don't say."

"It's about the will..."

"The will."

"Yes, the will. She had one drawn up after Curtis—after your father died." He took a long pause. I wanted to slap him to make him start talking and then slap him again to make him stop.

"...she left you the house and, well, the car."

"Gee, thanks, Mom."

Uncle Troy breathed deeply. "And she gave me and your Aunt

Lily custody of Beatrice."

Something black with spines dropped into my stomach. It was almost enough to make me double over.

"No way Troy. No fucking way."

"Jen, your Mom wanted what's best for you and Beatrice—"

"So she gets herself killed and sends my sister to live with you and Aunt Lily?" My voice shook.

"We'll take good care of her. You can live your life. Jesus, you're only twenty Jen, you don't want to be tied down."

"Like HELL I don't. Bug needs me. You've never even *had* kids. You don't know shit about Bug. Hell, you don't know shit about shit."

Uncle Troy cranked his face towards mine like he was ready to kill. My throat felt strangled. "It's fucking ending," I told him. "How can you say I can live my life when it's fucking over already?"

"Look," he said without sympathy, "the deal is that you have no choice. Furthermore, if you could think about your sister for one second instead of yourself you'd realize Aunt Lily and I have the resources for Beatrice's special needs. Resources, such as *money*, for one, that you don't have."

"All Bug needs is *me*. I've been there for her literally since day one. Trust me, she's fine."

Uncle Troy is shaking his head steadily. "Jen, my girl, no one's bought that line of crap for quite some time. I mean, Jesus Christ, she's twelve and she can't even walk right. At the very *least* she needs medication for those fits of hers."

"You don't think we tried meds? You don't think we had her looked at by every specialist and every two specialists they recommended? It was like a fucking hall of mirrors: no end in sight. No beginning, really, since no one could find anything that caused her development to —"

"— I'm well aware of what you all went through. I'm also aware that nothing has been done on this score for at least *six* years."

33

"Well, gee, I wonder if that has anything to do with my Dad kicking the bucket. Mom has her hands kind of full."

At the mention of my mother, Uncle Troy checked his watch.

"Had. Had her hands kind of full," he said.

That's when I decided not to talk to Uncle Troy anymore.

I wrap my arms around Bug. Her back is warm; her tender skin moves loosely over the slight suggestion of bone beneath. I put my cheek on hers and she presses her wet eyes into my neck. Maybe the closed casket confused her, maybe when Aunt Lily tutored her on fish scales she also tried to explain the concept of never and forever, and how in death they are ludicrously entwined. I don't know.

"Bug," I whisper into the curve of her ear, "Mommy is here and I am here. I'm sorry that we can't see Mommy like I said." I start rocking her, and she says something into my chest that I can't understand. "Do you want to go?" I ask. "Do you want to go home with me?" She doesn't answer and we just rock. We are drawn in, pulled together. I am scared now of our every heartbeat. I hold her tight. I don't know what to do. I could take her out to the hush of the foyer and calm her, or I could take her out the front door and keep walking. I hear the man at the podium shuffling his papers. I hear Aunt Lily's shallow, nervous breathing. I curl over my precious Bug and we rock, temporarily protected. Are we ready, I wonder, to leave Mom? Bug's wailing grows louder.

Stroking her hair, I turn to Uncle Troy. "We'll be right back," I say.

Diane M. Pitochelli

CIVILIZATION

And the name of the third river is Tigris:
the same passeth along by the Assyrians.
And the fourth river is Euphrates.
Genesis 2

When the rare
exquisite distance from
Sun to Earth placed
precious Life in
precarious balance;
When all seemed
bright with promise
in Eden;

the waves
ride to the shore
and die.

Where inventions
Apollonian and Dionysian
heal or destroy; where
boundaries drawn awaken
deep tribal instincts and formed
battlelines spawn hatreds; then

cavalries of moon-mad waves,
wild winds whip stallions galloping, manes
tangling,
crash violent
on black granite rocks;
sink to their knees
in sandstorms on shore.
 Some cry
  to the winds,
   'nevermore,'
 some sigh,
   'evermore.'

Leaving mewling
white gulls, circling violet-shrouded
skies; leaving mothers' fingertips running
over names, sandblasted
in black granite walls;

 the waves
  ride to the shore

     and die

Diane M. Pitochelli

WILLIAM SWEET WILLIAM

Superstar Will, "Sweet Swan of Avon"
I've come to praise you brother
your peppery swagger ... you inventive father of drama
your blushing cheeks ... you lyrical mother of poetry
your crocodile tears ... you player sister of the stage
I'll not bury you in shrill screams
like other groupies do, nor will I swoon
nor feign some flattery, for who needs to?

   [*Aside to strolling minstrel*]
 Boy, play a tune gaily on your lute
sing in dulcet tones for the master...
fast now he's exiting stage left.
   [*She beckons to the bard*]
Will, come back and sit here if you will
upon this Elizabethan throne downstage.
   [*Reenter the lead player William Shakespeare*]
Ah, a velvet pillow to rest that head my liege where twirls
and drones the teeming voices of all the world:
the wise, the clown, the shrew, the coy young thing,
the near insane, the mock hero, the ghost, the murderous villain,
the soothsayer, the traitor, the doomed lover, the forest fairy, the tragic
king,
the bastard, the first witch, the scheming queen, the third plebian.

Hear out my simple soliloquy would you Will?
I'll improvise briefly, so as not to try your patience to the end.
Put aside that worn down artificer quill for now.

Do you have to scribble night and day?
 [*Aside*] Always the urge to dramaturge.

[*She lifts a wooden goblet covered in tinfoil.*]
First a toast to the plots in every play,

 [*Aside*] though some purloined, all brilliant in some way.
and to the settings that mesmerize us in place: graveyards, battle fields,
moonlit forest, ladies chambers, gloomy castles, stormy moors.
and those unpropitious props: daggers, skulls, monarch crowns,
magic potions, beating drums, sounding trumpets, and striking clocks.
And here's to the throbbing passion in your sonnets
full of the foibles that foil us all
full of lies dressed as truth and truth disguised as lies
laced with the revolving seasons, cycles and circles of life
and the knotted darker secrets that make for thorny love.

 [*Aside*] He leaves now in a fog…not hearing me
following some thought … chasing a new line.
I'm doubly humbled in trying trippingly to tell him,
this prince of words; he sees through every soul and psyche
 [*Exit the balding bard*]
 [*Aside to the audience*] I'll cry out after him.
Adieu, farewell Sweet Will!
I prithee, will you at least give me credit for my good will?
 [*Roll the credits*] Alas, my name is nowhere to be seen.

Diane M. Pitochelli

IMPROVIZATION

Snaz pizzazz the spring green jazz of life
the somnambulant bazaar of everyday life
razz razzmatazz, the TV ads
the phone hawkers, fast talkers
the swift flashes of fads
masked rider politic insinuendoes
the rockers, the mockers
the melodious flights of raucous crows
the racing gracenotes of Rift Valley gazelles
the trumpeting elephants
warning the near-death of a nation
in syncopation
the drummer's hi-hat beats
the pianist's flying-fingers-feats
cymbalism floatation

The subconscious rathskeller of life
the synaptic connections of everyday life
the snap of an over stretched elastic band
the snapshot of the Tunisian desert sand
with the coal-fired train sizzled inert
goat herds and shepherds stare from low cliffs
in the surround sound of the kitchen's domestic riffs
the wild hum of a fridge on the blink
the dishwasher clatter by the cool stainless steel sink
the hot tea kettle whistling a reminder
the ding of the two-minute egg timer
the clank of the pipes
the growl of the dog at the plumber
the weed-whacker-lawn-mower-roar-roar-roar

devouring a morning's peace once more
the crash of tin in the recycle bin
tintinnabulation one more time again

The razzle-dazzle noise of modernity
pasted like wallpaper on psyche's internity
go embrace the silence and the serenity
in the woods or chapel at the monastery
escape to the sea and embrace the immensity
crash with the waves or surf virtually
escape to sip an espresso years ago
the unheard snore in broad daylight's glow
at the outdoor Café in Firenze
solar somniferous lazy
on Piazza della Signoria at noon
domani domani, la vita bella tune
Swingin' in the groove of life
the crowded labyrinthine soul of life
sooner or later the cell phone
the jazzman's wailing saxophone
the soothsayer
the naysayer
the child's prayer
a memory of skating the Zeider Zee
was it a child in a story or me?
from the first gig
to the last jig
and all in between
life is all dazzle
when you let in the sheen
spang spang-a-lang spang-a-lang

John Downey

CAMP AMBROSIA

Michael was the official new kid in school when I first met him in second grade. No one wanted to know anything about this kid, since they didn't want to be on the receiving end of a beatdown. It wasn't that he was big or mean; he just gave it off all around him. There was that way he walked, with his arms swinging loosely about his hips, that made you feel that he cared nothing for appearances. Or his mannerisms in conversation, spitting out his answers as though it was killing him to do so. Or his hair, never long enough to warm the back of his head or reach his ears, making you pictures every infamous terrorist in existence. (I heard that he did it himself, but I didn't believe it until I saw it for myself.)

All that seemingly disappeared, though, when he was called on that fateful day in April 2000, a week after he moved to Andover, to tell the class what he would do when he grew up.

"I want to rule the world."

Many snickered; a few gave questioning looks; several laughed. I smiled.

Our teacher, for her part, regarded him as though Michael had said doctor or movie star or fireman (Rod Cersings', Finnigan Langdon's, and Jacob Dziedzic's answers, respectively. Strange how I can remember that detail, but not the name of the teacher.) That only made her follow-up more amusing.

"Why do you want to rule the world, Michael?"

"Well, I want to do something that leaves a mark in the world. When you're a doctor or something like that, all the stuff you do is boring and dull, and it doesn't leave anything behind for my kids. I mean, look at yourself. When you were growing up, did you want some job that makes you want to tie your tubes and never get married?"

I guess I should have seen it then, but at the time, I thought it was just a joke.

At this point our teacher probably figured, *Maybe if he keeps talking, he'll top himself.* So she asked, "How will you take over the world, Michael?

"Well, first I'll start with killing the President, then I'll say I'm Prez before anyone else can, then declare war on South America, Africa, Europe, Antarctica – "

The rest I didn't hear; the room was filled with giggles, full-blown laughs from all sides of the room. Finnigan Langdon, who was usually the one dishing out the jokes, fell out of his seat laughing. Yes, I laughed my butt off, I'll admit.

But then our teacher did something that set off a new chapter in my life, and the lives of many other Andover children as well: She told him his plan was impossible.

"It's called 'order of succession.' You'll learn about it next year."

The look on Michael's face as he returned to his seat said it all. It was of simultaneous panic, sadness, and embarrassment. Had he truthfully believed that it was going to be his job when he grew up? Apparently so, as no sooner had I turned away from him than his butt missed his seat by a good six inches, setting off another laughfest. We were happy that day, I guess.

He sat next to me in every class I had, but we didn't speak for the longest time. This was not for lack of trying, though; I have always lived by the words "People should be judged as harmful to be around only when they have proved undeniably so" (It sounds a lot shorter in my head.), and I tried to pry conversations out of him every other day. "Nice weather" was batted away with "Your point being…?"; "Good try" was deflected by "But it's still wrong"; "Aren't all mothers weird?" prompted "Evil is more like it"; et cetera, et cetera, etc.

In fact we didn't have a single conversation until the second week in May, and Michael was the one who started it. "Is it wrong to want to take over the world?"

"Um…what?"

"Is it?"

"Well…it's more strange than it is wrong."

"Yeah, but all the other jobs are for pansies. Dictator – now there's a job. Meet lots of people, have an opinion that matters, let those who deserve to live do so…"

I regarded him as Hitler-in-blue-jeans. He was starting to get a little worked up, so I deflected the topic, not necessarily changing it, but pointing it in the "right" direction. "But it looks like you can't do that now, right?"

"I've been thinking about how it's possible. 'Cause it is."

"Explain."

"Well, first I would need an army from somewhere, anywhere at all. With that army, I would take another country over and get their troops, and then another country, and so on, until all the nations of the world are under my grasp."

"Well, where's your army?"

"That's the problem." I gave an extended glance at Michael's desk and, for the first time, could read what he wrote and understand it.

~~Denmark~~ where?

~~France~~ speak French

~~USA~~ take over last

~~Antarctica~~ run by people in fur coats – not good against Mexico

~~Mexico~~ too far away

This classroom

~~My family~~

Greenland

~~Africa~~ has too many problems

~~England~~ pansies

"There are no good armies left for me."

"I see you haven't crossed out two of your choices."

"What? Oh, that. Well, I talked to my dad about it, and he said that those two were the only ones left for me."

Rick Smith turned around and said, "Well, what about Canada?"

"Nah. Dumb people."

"No, they're actually very smart, according to my uncle. They're also very nice, too.

"You mean pansy nice?"

"No I mean scary nice. As in feeling so bad about stealing $50 from you they give you $200."

"Pansies, though."

"Pansies with guns. My uncle goes hunting every season, and he says everyone there has a gun."

"Uptight nice pansies?"

"Laid back nice pansies with guns. Seriously, if anyone wanted to take advantage of that…"

"All right. So my army is Canadian."

He then shut up for a second, at which point I finally interjected something: "But how are you going to take over Canada?"

The bell rang, signaling the end of the school day. Michael said, "I'll figure it out. Just watch."

And he went home.

The next day, everything felt new. My whole schedule was off. I was dizzy. Discombobulated. The ride to school was on a different road than I was used to – gravel and potholes where a smooth grind should have been. The effort to hide my discomfort from my friends almost made me vomit. But I managed.

Michael seemed not to care about my condition. "I figured it out."

I said, with surprisingly no frog in my throat, "That fast?"

"Do I have anything better to do? I've got it all figured out." Ms. So-and-so told us class was beginning, so we quieted down.

At the midday bell, he said we'll discuss it at lunch. "But first, I have to go to the nurse's office. Save me a seat!"

On the walk there, I ran into Jeremy.

He said hi, I said hi. He said how's it going, I said I'm trying. He said it was a tough choice, and I said nothing. He said it's for the best, and I ran to the bathroom so that my tears couldn't be seen.

Like I said, I managed.

Fortunately, Michael had a lot to say. He got so worked up in his ideas, he attracted a group of kids from every table around him. It was like watching those televangelists on TV reaching out to hopeful minds.

"What I NEED…is your support. The support…of a select few. Some may perish, some…may get hurt. BUT…those who succeed will not have to work a day in their lives!"

Sorry if I misled you, but I had not heard the first part of his long-winded speech; his trip to the nurse's office had been far shorter than my crying spell. In fact, it was at about the end of his speech that I walked in.

When he saw me, he gave his crowd a scowl, and a very sizable number of his audience scattered, leaving me a seat across from him. As soon as I sat down, he laid out a map of the United States and pointed to Massachusetts, his finger covering practically the entire state.

"What we need is food, money, flints, clothes, and people."

My response was an intelligent "Huh?" Yeah, I was out of it there.

"Lots of all those things. Drinks too. But mostly people. That's something we need the most. And these guys here are loyal enough, tough enough, good enough to make it."

He drew a line from Massachusetts to the southern tip of Canada, avoiding large bodies of water, as I examined this group. Finnigan Langdon. Rod Cersings. Jacob Dziedzic. Rick Smith. Kevin Sortings. Damon Kurack. Stephen Mentz. 'Little' John Panamalosioniote. 'Big' John Himes. Terry Zerowitz. And James Nixon. Quite a strange group, I had to say.

"…and then, at that part, we end up in Canada, and we'll figure it out from there."

"Excuse me," Little John piped in, "but I have two questions."

"Go ahead."

"One, shouldn't we figure out where we are going while in Canada now?"

"Good point. What cities are in Canada?"

"Ottawa, Montreal, Calgary, British Columbia, Toronto – "

"Toronto sounds the coolest. Next question."

"OK, how are we going to convince our parents to drive us to Canada so we can take it over?"

"We 're walking there, dummy. Look how close it is! It'll take no time at all!"

"But we'll need to take over Canada before our parents figure it out, or they will just take us home."

"Well, then, we'll simply need to find a way to fool them for a really long time."

"How?"

Michael opened his mouth to speak, but he stopped himself. He hadn't thought of parents at all, and now the entire plan was in jeopardy.

My answer surprised even myself. "Summer camp. Tell your parents you're going to summer camp with a few friends. A camp with rules against writing letters, phone calls, e-mail, parents visiting, or anything that would allow us to contact the outside world."

Little John said, "What if they won't let us?"

"Beg a lot."

"But –"

"If they want to take you there, say you're riding with a friend."

Then someone – I forget who – raised the point of naming the camp, in case our parents called each other to verify the name. We didn't think that they would call each other to see if the person who drove them to camp actually did that, or anything else, but that wasn't the issue. A name for the camp would seal the deal in our minds, make sure that our parent would never be an issue.

Finnigan suggested Campdogdoo, hoping for a chuckle, but this was a serious issue, and he got no reaction at all. Jacob Dziedzic chimed in, "What about Camp Fairgrounds?" which prompted Michael to yell "NO!" in such a way that we knew we had touched something he didn't want touched. Terry Zerowitz came up with the best name, Camp Ambrosia, which everyone thought had a nice ring to it.

"All right," said Michael, "anything else? Anything at all?"

James raised his hand. "Um, yeah, uh, Mikey-"

"Michael."

"Yeah, um, my sister might, uh, come along with us."

Silence. Not an "Oh, man, that stinks" silence. Or a "What are we supposed to say" silence. We were just waiting to see what Michael would do.

Finally, Michael said, "No."

"That may not be up to me, though."

"Why?"

"'Cuz she'll find out, she'll figure it out, and she'll want to come, I know her - "

"Don't let her."

"I'll try, Mikey, really I will - "

"My name is Michael."

"Um, yeah, I'll try, but she'll figure it out, she always does."

"Whatever. I don't want to have to kill anybody to eat their flesh because someone ate all our food."

Understand that cannibalism is funny to a bunch of grade school kids, and you can understand our laughter. Not a full-blown, people-falling-0over laughfest like the one the month before, just a few giggles. But it lightened our mood nevertheless.

"Let's go outside," Finnigan said, and we did.

I had to separate myself from the rest of the crew to have some time for myself, to collect my thoughts. Most of the time, this was not a distressing exercise, but on this day it was. The first thought in my mind was *How could Jeremy say that to me?* The second was *I told you so, you shouldn't have gotten your hopes up like that, bad things happen when life is perfect, what goes up must come down…*

The third was *I wonder what Canada looks like.*

Danny Henriquez

OUT OF THE LIGHT

I want to step off the stage
away from the spotlight.
Be invisible to the audience;
walk through the aisles where people stand.
I see the people waving,
but not at me
They can't see me
as I walk by the tombstones;
all of them the color of cement.

Danny Henriquez

FATBOY

It was late on a Saturday night. I was chilling at the movies with my friends. After the movies we were in the theater parking lot. Then twenty minutes later a dark green Acura approached us. It had the light on low, almost off. The car was going very slow. It must have been going about five miles an hour. As the car got closer and closer, my friends and me grew more curious to know who was in it.

Finally, the car stopped right next to us. When the tinted windows rolled down all I could see was a dark-skinned guy. Next to him was a light-skinned guy. The dark-skinned guy asked us, "Who do you represent?" We answered, "Nobody." I could barely swallow, and my heartbeat raced faster and faster. Then out of nowhere he pulled out a gun. It was a black twenty-two millimeter with a chrome top. It looked like my father's gun.

I dropped to the ground. Then I heard two shots. It sounded like a whole bunch of firecrackers going off. As soon as the car left, I stood up. I touched my chest and my stomach. I saw no blood on me, and I didn't feel any pain, so I knew I wasn't shot. Then Jairo yelled out, "Yo, Danny. Fatboy got shot, son!" The first thing that came to my mind was Damn! I couldn't believe what had just happened. I got up and ran to Fatboy and Jairo. I got down on my knees and held Fatboy's head up. He just stared at me and said, "Danny, you are my true friend. Anybody would have just ran and left me here, but you didn't."

I gave Jairo my cell and told him to call 911. I was nervous and mad, but at the same time I felt paranoid. I couldn't even think straight. When the ambulance came, I watched

Fatboy in disbelief. I saw his chest full of blood. He was even bleeding in his mouth. He lay on the ground holding his chest. He looked at me, and as the paramedics picked him up, he said, "Danny, you my boy, and if I die, take care and don't become a gangsta, son." I said, "Nah, son, you can't die on me now. He said, "Don't worry. I'll watch from the heavens."

I think back and say to myself that God still loves me because I didn't die that day. I believe that Fatboy is looking down on me right now. I know he's looking at me with a smile on his face because he's guiding me on the right path. I followed his words and didn't become a gangsta. I stayed away from drugs. I've never been arrested. I'm clean. I still go to school because I consider that to be the right path. Rest in peace, Paylala, a.k.a. Fatboy.

Tara L. Masih

THE BURNINGS

I work hard in the dormant month of February to remind myself of the warmth and life and light all being stored up in the surrounding woods and earth and animals. But this February I am interrupted by the exit of one life.

I watch, from my bay window, cardinals forage for seed in the brown grass beneath the shepherd's crook. The brilliant-feathered male pushes the female away. She hops back at a respectful distance, unperturbed, I think. She must know that in just a few months her mate will once again be feeding her in courtship.

When Lenore first comes into the living room to tuck a knitted afghan around my arthritic knees, I don't see she is crying. Then a small catch of her breath takes me away from the scene outside.

"Ethel called . . . Linda is gone."

"Gone?"

Lenore backs up without looking behind until she reaches the couch, then falls into it. "A few days ago. Liver disease. She kept it a secret, how bad she was. The funeral's tomorrow."

I've noticed, in recent years, that the tears on my wife's good face no longer fall--they meander through the creases, find rest in flat rivulets that begin at her eyes, eyes of a blue no longer intense but soft and comforting.

"Do ya hear me, Donald?" she asks after a silence I know she judges to be too long.

"I hear you." When my wife gets upset, her brogue grows stronger.

The cardinals fly off in unison when the sudden turn of my head in the window reflection startles them. Or maybe it is Judith, my neighbor to the right, crossing the tree-line of white pines, plastic container in hand.

"Damn it, Lenore, she's doing it again--taking my seed!"

Judith tilts the tube feeder and gathers the millet and sunflower seed mixture into her container, then takes small, guilty, elfin steps back to her property.

The afghan slides to the floor. "I'm calling her this time. She's emptied half the feeder!"

Lenore sighs, wipes her face first with her fingertips, then with the backs of her hands. "Just let it be, Donald, just let *her* be."

I wait by the car for my wife to check the stove and leave the house. The winter sky looks vast, a gray ocean. I reach to the car for ballast--a touch of vertigo for a moment, a feeling of insignificance.

We are becoming used to late-night phone calls and the sad, necessary flurry of funeral preparations. But this time, the death of our friend and neighbor's daughter, Linda, hits harder. A life not fully lived, both in years and accomplishments, is harder to celebrate.

I can't help but think about my own daughter, who used to play with Linda in a tree house her father and I erected in the woods between our two properties. If Melissa had just left me now, forever, I would never look at the world as whole again. It would always be a treacherous puzzle, with the most important piece missing. Lenore would feel the same--she had immediately rushed to the phone to call Melissa, ostensibly to tell her the news, but I knew the mother needed to affirm that the daughter hadn't somehow disappeared, too.

The North Parish church lot is crowded with mourners. We are directed to the last row of seats, handed programs for the service.

"Her ex-husband is giving the eulogy," Lenore whispers.

I glance at the name she points to, printed in uneven typewriter font. "They divorced, what, ten years ago?"

"He's over there."

But I'm looking to my friend, Rowan, in the first row. I hear some heavy words like "pain" and "alcoholism" during the service, and move to escape the church's old, overactive heaters.

The ground outside is uneven, frost-heaved. The stones that frame the church are large, chiseled granite taken from parish land. They have been hewn into a strong, seemingly sturdy house of worship. I study the dry moss and ochre-tinged lichen that discolors the mortar, which cements the rocks that will outlast all of those they house.

Lenore returns from her lunch with that cold, sweet smell of winter air about her. I'm fixing a barley stew for dinner, and it has to bake in the oven for several hours. I ease a knife into a mushroom, slice it in half.

Lenore puts a carrot piece into her mouth and chews carefully. "That was hard. Ethel cried a lot, but I think she needed to."

"Where did you go?"

"Palmers. We didn't really eat, but it looked good . . . soup and salad."

"We're having stew tonight."

"Thanks. . . . Donald?"

"Hmmm?"

"You should talk to Rowan. Ethel says he won't talk to her. She thought maybe, you being a man, and a friend--"

"Oh, hon, what would I say?"

"Don't say anything. Listen."

I point to the red cooking wine next to the stove. She hands it to me so I can pour it into the simmering pot.

"What if he doesn't talk? Doesn't want to? Sometimes talk makes things worse."

Lenore puts her fists on her hips, elbows out--as she does when she's frustrated with me—and shakes her head slowly.

"Donald MacIntyre. Just be a good friend, okay? He's gonna do some burnin' tomorrow, you go see him."

"I've got nothing left to burn this season."

"Then *make* somethin' ta burn," she snaps, as chilly as the evening that's coming on.

The cozy smell of a wood fire wends its way down from the hill above our land. Pushed by a bone-chilling wind, it enters the cracks around my old, four-paned windows. Lenore comes into the living room a second time, stares at me in an effort to get me moving.

I put down the book I've been pretending to read for several hours, unable to concentrate on the gardening tool chapter.

"I'll go, I'll go."

I gear up for the cold, pull on a knit cap, and set out into the backyard to find something to burn.

I find the end-of-winter landscape so unalluring. The cold covers all natural scents, and life contracts into itself, waiting, biding its time. The sounds of animal calls still hold, though: the flock of crows that caws when it sees me, their sharp eyes looking to my hands for the whiteness of stale bread; the nattering of alarmed squirrels, amidst creaking limbs; the scream of a red-tailed hawk, and the cacophony of the crows now in pursuit.

Nature, I think, has a temper. Last night it was angry, lashing about. Some old oak branches were thrown to the ground, both black with rot and white with fungus. One lies stuck, like a broken arm, having plunged end first into our lawn. Still, they are not enough to burn.

My eyes fall on the picnic bench sitting patiently under the pines, the trees lacy from the loss of needles. The bench leans to the left, its surface seamed and weathered like silver driftwood. In summertime you'll see moss growing in cracks, and little red fungus that looks like tiny, haphazard bunches of "lollipop trees," as Melissa calls them.

Without hesitation, I unlock the tool shed and pull out the axe. I hit hard, taking time to rest during the slow, steady attack.

The red wheelbarrow squeaks through the dry, shrunken undergrowth. I push it over scrub and dormant vines of wild strawberry, sumac, and deadly nightshade. Rowan and I have slowed in our quest to keep the woods between our homes clear of the kinds of small, weedy greenery that impedes progress. His side is especially overgrown since he began summering in Maine--front lawn overtaken by myrtle, rhododendrons, tall grasses, and towering pines. I force the barrow through the trees, aiming for the hot orange light flashing between trunks.

He looks up when I enter the clearing, his eyes hidden behind glasses that reflect his bonfire. The two round, flickering globes hide his expression. He is in a circle of cardboard boxes and green trash bags.

"Smelled the burning, had this old picnic table to get rid of." I begin to feed the flames with the old cedar axed into three-foot sections. The fire embraces the wood, sucks out what's left of its life like a vampire, and tosses its ash to the sky. While I say a silent farewell to the bench that once supported my family during picnics, absorbed our beer and lemonade, Rowan carefully, gently, gives the fire what I soon realize are letters--papers of different colors, faded pinks and yellows, colors of our daughters' youths, those boldly drawn daisies and perfect round dots of the sixties and early seventies decorating some of them.

They all burn the same way--corners to center.

He opens one envelope, a plain white one, pulls out the yellow, legal-size paper, and reads to himself. "It's from me," he says. "It's a letter I wrote to her after her divorce, asking her to get help." He raises his right thumb and forefinger to his glasses, efficiently wipes away the tears gathering in the corners.

"I have to go through all her stuff now. Ethel can't do it. Her clothes I took down to the Salvation Army. I took her books to the library. But what do I do with these personal things? So much paper . . . I can't watch the garbage truck take them away."

He slides the letter back into its envelope, hesitates for a moment, then drops it into the fire. The flames feed off wood and paper, growing hotter, forcing us back. Fire is so fascinating because it looks alive. It almost speaks to me. Mesmerized, I stare. I hear flames, loud as thunder, screams.

Cautiously, I remember. "I used to live in New York, before my folks moved to Haverhill." I pause, letting my mind refill with long-buried memories and feelings. "You remember May 6, 1937? Also my birthday. I'd finally gotten that BB gun from Hammond's storefront window. And I remember it was a gray day, storming over New Jersey. I was out playing with my gun, and suddenly there was this, this silver balloon on the horizon, growing larger and larger. It passes over the Newson farm. I see ribbed sides . . . huge, black-and-white swastikas in a red square, flag flying from the tail . . . mooring ropes curving down from its nose. The hum of engines is really loud. It passes overhead, this *huge,* stately bird. It covers my view of the sky. I take aim . . . *Bam!*"

"You shot at the *Hindenberg?*" Rowan is listening, his hands in his front jacket pockets. I bring my arms back down from their frozen, raised position.

"I heard the broadcast on Dad's Gabriel Heater radio that night. The announcer's voice broke. Sounds of death and disaster. *My* disaster. I killed those people, I thought. . . I buried my BB gun; lived, years, with my secret. It was only when I got old enough to know a BB couldn't reach that far that I could accept not being responsible. Can you believe that, though? I really thought I was responsible."

Rowan's mouth shows the crack of a smile, like light under a door. He shakes his head. "You stupid son-of-a-bitch."

I stay with Rowan a while longer. We empty boxes and bags together as ceremoniously as possible. The last paper is tossed, and he shakes his head again, slaps me on the back. I hear something released in his laugh, and the sound, like an animal cry, goes up into the trees and gets caught and tossed around in their outreaching, comforting limbs.

Scout Kingery

HOW I REMEMBER JACK

The big knife, rusted
and dull from years
of careless use, was
balanced, precariously,

on the tool shed wall.
Jack and I found it there,
balanced. Resting in the
musky room, heady

with oils and fertilizer.
Drunk with eight-year-old fantasy,
we flew low through wheat,
chopping and soaring

down slopes of ivy.
Jungles we created consumed us
until we were called
back to the house,

back to warm milk and cold sandwiches,
showers, wet hair, and television.

Scout Kingery

WITH COOL FEET IN THE WATER

Cool breezes of late June press against the lazy curves
        of the Mutton Mountains

and shoot across the water, through the trees, birch and dogwood
        that live on soft back-eddies,

to the nettles, by our swimming hole
        where we keep melons cold on hot days.

As the nettles, with their little teeth, flex and bow
        in the afternoon light

a salmon fly gets whisked into the ripples
        created by slick stones the color of trout.

The little body flails on its way down to the current, writhing,
        flashing hopelessly against the breeze

a magnificent orange, quickly muted
        by the cool ripples.

How is it that this fly, my fly, could rest
        content in nettles only to be launched, ultimately,

by something so beautiful as a June breeze
        to the silent current

and get snapped up by a trout
        the color of slick river rocks?

Scout Kingery

DOVE HUNT

Every year on August 31st we drive down the dusty old grade.
down to the Deschutes,
down to the desert.
Down to where fields of green alfalfa live mutually
with the dry dearth of color.
For a few days we enjoy the serenity,
to be interrupted only by shots in the distance
or the noisy rafters floating through.
Days are long—filled with masculine beauties:
fishing and hunting, a poker game on the second night
and riding, though the tack still hangs
unmoved from the hooks.

At dawn on the 1st, the season starting,
having piled into one car, a little coffee
and the touch of cold steel and walnut
is enough to get us going.
Past fishing holes and rapids.
Past the barn and the horses.
Past the fields of alfalfa, brooding without the sun.
Up to the springs, ready to hike,
wearing bright hats and dark clothes,
with Brownings and shells, we walk heavy,
through air charged with juniper and sage.

We post around a young creek, watching the colors
grow with the morning light,
crouched. Ready
with chambers locked and senses sharp.
"Mark!"
3 small birds sweep through the gauntlet of sleepy hunters.
I swing my barrel through them and squeeze the trigger.

Paul Marion

MAJESTIK LINEN

In a subterranean room roaring like a jet,
Sunday workers feed or unload machines,
busy in twos and threes at their stations —
all hands more colorful than the linen.
Plain as old-time mill operatives, they handle cloth by the mile:
nursing home pillow cases, dinner napkins, green scrubs
   from the ER,
loved sheets, double-bleached butchers' aprons, hotel towels,
well-fed tablecloths from a club luncheon.
The linen workers take it in and send it on — their canvases
   unsigned.
A young woman catches my face in the window.
Instead of giving her a wave, any kind of salute,
I freeze like a common eavesdropper.
She turns back to her work, what most of us won't see
unless we're in the Flats at the hour of the early Mass,
following the drone of automatic washers
to a sunrise service recognized worldwide.
Their names are in the phone book with ours.
We get the job done. We know the drill by heart.
We press and fold the linen before it is loaded onto trucks,
bound for back doors across the city.

Paul Marion

PARLEZ-VOUS?

Pierre Bouchard's sports-talk radio show
finds its way from Montreal to my room,
the chatty French fading in and out;
I'm picking up key words, leaning towards
the Panasonic Solid-State portable.
In the dark I reached over to fine-tune
a Boston station and on the signal's edge
caught a Canadian phone call in mid-flight —
the cold clear December air a blue net,
the stars like a connect-the-dots game
transmitting my root tongue,
language of those who carried my name down
and down through Quebec backwoods, villages,
down through New England hills,
down through pine-cone valleys
to this mill town whose brick factories
make a great red wall along the river.
Bouchard and his callers talk football, hockey;
a commercial praises lovely Montreal,
Paris of North America, cosmopolitan hive.
They wish each other "Joyeux Noël,"
voices blinking slowly like fancy tree lights.

Paul Marion

NEW PINE HILL

"On this site grew the heart of the Franco-American community. Hard working French-Canadians came to fill the mills of Lowell and build a tradition of faith, generosity, and pride."
—Little Canada Memorial

Mr. Alphonse Hudon, wearing a blue parka and dress hat, leans on his cane on Pawtucket Street, checking the freshly tarred walk and grove of short pines along the Northern Canal. "Looks good, doesn't it?" I ask. And he says, "I liked it better the way it was," which opens up a line of talk, because I know he's missing the French Canadian-American village that once colored this shoulder of land at the wide bend in the river. I tell him my father, Marcel, was raised on Cheever Street in what was their Little Canada. And he says he knew my father and grandfather, Wilfrid, whose meat market filled a corner at Austin and Moody. He corrects me on the address of Marquis' garage, where my dad had our family car serviced before the wrecking cranes pulled up. I recall a house across the street with a tree poking through the front porch roof. "Oh, yes," he says, "that was Mr. Marquis' house. And there was a monkey there, too."

The black-and-white sign on the canal bridge reads: "Jean-Paul Frechette — The Blond Tiger," with the boxer's two dates underneath. Another remnant, like the Little Canada memorial, bronze plaque mounted on a granite stone "from one of the last blocks to be torn down," placed by Franco-Americans and the priests of St. Jean Baptiste parish, now a Latino Catholic church, Nuestra Señora Del Carmen. There's a fleur-de-lis in each corner, beginning and end dates, 1875 – 1964, like a gravestone, like one life, and a litany of streets running up the sides: Aiken, Cabot, Cheever, Coolidge, Hall, Melvin, Montcalm, Pawtucket, Perkins, Suffolk, Tucker, Ward. The amen is Quebec's motto, Je Me Souviens! — Lest We Forget!

All that history and geography in a supersaturated marker, tucked between evergreens on Aiken Street, in the middle of what was once a district so dense only Hell's Kitchen beat it. You stuck an arm out the window to touch the next tenement. You heard one tongue for blocks. People ate, slept, drank, and dreamt in a native sound arranged like code. Rag man, icebox, coal chute, baseball. Pork pie, baked beans, mill rat, whiskey. High Mass, soirée, L'Étoile, soupe rouge.

What was here is what Mr. Hudon liked better, a familiar world that seemed to work for people who got up in the morning with something to do. Even I remember, though I was a kid when Urban Renewal clear-cut the blocks. The way he looked down the long canal made me want to say something hopeful. I admire the young trees, the sweeping path, whose design takes us to the manmade channel and black water that still moves the wheels.

The rough, stubby foundation stone is a local version of the monolith from *2001: A Space Odyssey*, the one that made the monkeys go ape, the one the moon-men couldn't figure, the floating answer-bar. This hunk of rock on Earth states its case for the record, like the metal message boards shipped out with satellites, telling somebody out there who we are.

Bobby Carleo

MODERN LIVING

This is the desolate wilderness of life as a chimera
Sown by God (fate, chance)
torn by backroads, sidewalks, and bikepaths...
A broken tapestry ...in it a leaf falls
leaves
(and how the tears come!)

At midnight I drink in abandoned parking lots and try
pulling myself together
...dissecting the face in the mirror
(it is covered, of course, in tears)
to determine its innermost, truest desires.
— If I have to,
I will sow them myself
(and if I do, I'll attach the leaf).

Bobby Carleo

THE BURNING ONSET OF LATENCY

We looked up and saw the sky, darker now, softened, dampened, and breathing the coming purity of night. Low and a little to the left wonderful colors shot over the hills. Life seemed sent forth to us, as a gift; inside me swelled and proliferated happiness—and I felt obliged to turn away and give it back. Possibly I felt I didn't deserve it, but I doubt that was it. Instinctively rejecting something so innocent and pleasing is horribly unjust. I might have felt different if I couldn't have taken it for granted, but I could have—at least that's the way I felt—so I was stuck feeling stupid at being unhappy because I was happy.

"Do you remember at the end of *Brave New World*?" I asked her, and she looked over at me. "When the Savage won't appreciate anything he has." I paused. "Or appreciates it too much. Or something. I don't know." I looked back out over the horizon.

"Yeah."

"Do you ever feel that way?" I didn't move, and listened closely.

"I think so."

I kept looking forward, and thought for a minute. "Did you finish it?"

She gave me a strange look. "The book?"

"Yeah."

"Yeah."

"Oh—I never did. I never read the last few pages."

"That's funny."

"I know. I wanted to, I just never got around to it." I accidentally let in an instant of uncomfortable silence. "Don't tell me what happens, though. I want to read it someday. It'll be interesting, cause I've wondered for so long."

She smiled quietly and breathed a laugh, maybe out of pity, possibly awkwardness. I thought it was strange but was glad for it anyways. I couldn't really take it for granted.

"I love you," she said, somehow naturally despite everything. The inside of me jumped, and I felt electric and scared.

I sighed slowly out loud as though making myself comfortable, to help me relax, and because I needed to cushion my attempt to respond. "I love you, too."

Indeterminate pause.

"I don't understand," she confessed.

"Me neither," I told her.

Strangest sunset ever.

Peggy Rambach

First Chapter from

THE LONS

a novel-in-progress

I

There wasn't much more he could do. He'd irrigated them, he'd fertilized them and now he kicked one. "Grow," he said.

The watermelon shuddered and lay still. And something about the movement made Leonard look closer. It had seemed not to come from the impact of his boot, but from the melon itself. Then he heard a general shuffle of leaves and he could have sworn that it had been caused by the same little movement from all the melons in the field. He glanced up but the field was as still as it had been when he'd looked down.

"Huh," Leonard said, took off his baseball cap, wiped his forehead with his forearm, and put the cap back on.

The watermelons that by now should have been fully mature and ready to harvest, were the size of wiffle balls and just about as light. And though Leonard Slinket had been growing his "lons" as he called them, and selling them for years, by the honor system, in a little stand built roadside in front of his house, he had to say, he'd never seen anything like this.

Now he squatted, inspecting the one he'd kicked, like he'd inspected any one of them a million times before, for fungus, for rot. He'd even called the seed company a week ago to see if there'd been a mix-up in their packaging or distribution and they'd mistakenly sent him a dwarf strain.

But the plant looked perfectly healthy. The leaves were broad and thick, if more turquoise in color than he'd have associated with a melon plant. And the lons were firm and striped the usual two-toned green and they gleamed like they'd been individually polished. But then, looking closer, he saw something he hadn't seen before. The vine that one was attached to, he could have sworn, was moving. Not like a snake or worm or anything. It was something so subtle and slight, he had to touch it to be sure. And there it was, a pulse as strong and steady as it would have been had it come from the thump thump thump of a healthy human heart.

"Holy -" Leonard said, and stood up fast, then stepped back and felt the heel of his boot catch on the vine behind him. He swung out his arms, threw his weight forward, but he fell anyway, hard, and felt something collapse beneath him with the small explosive sound of a lightbulb.

For a moment Leonard didn't move. He heard a crow caw and a car drive by on the road that bordered the field, and the sun was just as bright and hot as it had been moments earlier and the day before this one, so for a moment it felt to Leonard like nothing was different and there was nothing to be afraid of. At least not until he heard a humming sound which had the richness to it that could only be attributed to the fact that it emanated not from one source but from a multitude. It was the sound of an enormous choir. It was a sad sound, musical and dignified, like a dirge or a requiem. And the intensity made the leaves of the plants in front of him and to either side tremble.

Still, he didn't move, unprepared and unwilling, too transfixed by the deep and sorrowful sound all around him to get up and see what he had done. And then it stopped with the uniformity of an orchestra at the cut-off, and Slinket heard that same persistent crow and had to wonder again if he'd really heard anything at all.

But what he did not have to question, once he finally stood up and looked down, was that the thing he had so unceremoniously squashed, was nothing that had anything to do with a watermelon.

"John, I'm telling you, it looked like, well like something like an egg. I mean a broken egg, but without a shell. I mean more like, you know, like a frog's egg. The outside, it was hard, but not very and just under it was this kind of jelly. Blue jelly-like," he paused, holding the heavy black receiver, listening intently, " Yeah, like Jell-o. Blue Jell-o." He paused again and took off his baseball cap and rubbed his palm rapidly back and forth across his scalp, disrupting the strands of hair there that had previously been lying flat. Then he put his hat back on again and sighed. "You know – I don't like, I don't need you to make a joke of this. Listen. Just come on over here and take a look at the damn thing. I guarantee you this: you're not going to be making any Jell-o jokes then, I'll tell you."

Leonard hung up, then he looked somewhere in the middle of the kitchen floor. So what should he do now? He'd left the thing out in the field along with his nifty new Deering tractor because he'd right then and there stripped off his bluejeans, socks and boots and run in his skivvies right on up to the house and straight into the shower.

And then he'd scrubbed what had at first just felt warm, like the effects of a strong eucalyptus lineament, which had then increased in temperature to resemble that of a yellow jacket sting which had then intensified to feel like the sunburn he'd suffered on his one and only journey outside the U.S. border to Cancun Mexico, and then it had just gone away. Right away, as if at a finger snap. But since there seemed to be no symptom left of any sort from having suffered these sensations, not even a little tenderness back there, maybe his imagination had been working overtime, whatever was left of it anyway, because he wouldn't have denied that he hadn't really used it much since he'd won runner-up at his high school science fair something like forty years ago.

It had been odd, getting out of the shower midday, like he was sick or something. He only took showers at night, after he'd put in a day's work in his produce field and done the books for H&R's Men's Clothes, Montgomery Motors and Smith's Tire Company among other smaller businesses in town. Slinket had always been good with numbers and growing things, and knew very well what he was good at because he'd defined long ago what he wasn't good at: carpentry and women and, if he'd had the chance, most likely fatherhood.

Leonard had put on some clean pressed jeans and the kind of white button down shirt he'd have worn to a funeral or a party. His brush with the inexplicable today had made him want to look a little better, a little neater than usual. He didn't want John Bigby accusing him of being unbalanced just because he might have a few hairs awry and some stubble on his face – his usual appearance, he had to admit. So he'd carefully combed his hair into even stripes. He'd shaved. And he'd finally put to use Montgomery Motors' Christmas gift cologne.

"Well. Don't you look all spiffed up," John said. He stood outside the door looking good enough to be hired by UPS without the formality of an application. He was twenty-five years Leonard's junior, but just as tall, and so when they looked at each other, they could always look eye to eye even if they rarely saw it - mostly on issues relating to rapid growth of the town from that of a farming to a bedroom community - like property taxes, parking, leash laws and school expansion projects. Upon all these issues they were well known adversaries, but some might say their rather public display of disaffection was more for the love of debate and semantics than anything personal. In fact, Leonard had to admit that he was pretty glad to see Bigby at his door even if he did look like he'd stopped by for an afternoon of entertainment at his expense.

"So do you want to see it or not?"

"You're not even going to invite me in for a cup a coffee?"

"No." said Leonard.

John smiled. Blue eyes, black hair that showed no signs of vacating its original place of residence. The guy should have been in Hollywood, Leonard thought, feeling as usual irritated by that fact, yet still glad he'd shown up.

"Let's go then," Leonard said.

The tractor serving as a landmark, it didn't take much time for Leonard to spot the blue jean blue of the pants he had so quickly shimmied out of, still right where he'd left them, looking like the occupant had melted Wicked-Witch-of-the-West-style, boots stuck in the bottoms and socks still in the boots.

"You just got buck naked, here, Len?" said John.

"Not naked," Leonard said, "but you would've too, John, if you felt whatever the hell it was that I was feeling coming right through my pants."

"Uh huh." John said, smiling

"You would've," Leonard said.

"Okay, Len. I'll believe you," said John, who really did like Leonard, his irascibility, his fierce opposition to the inevitability of change. He was an old hold-out and he had to admire him for it in a grudging kind of way. Every town needed a Slinket.

Leonard bent over, and with thumb and forefinger pinched the very edge of the left leg of his pants, and at arms length, raised them from the ground like he would, had they been submerged in raw sewage. Then he swung his extended arm around like it was a construction crane and dropped them again at a safer distance. He left his workboots where they were, with his grayish socks poking out of them, then crouched down to see – well, not much. Now the little lon just looked like the remains of something that had been left for days at the high tide mark on a beach. Dry and leathery, brown-green in color and flat as a punctured plastic playground ball. And strangest thing of all, it smelled like something a seagull would pick at. The leaves had withered black and crispy, and the vine looked like it had been salt preserved. "Well it was – Well, you can't say it looks like a watermelon, now can you?" he said.

"No, you can't," John said slowly. He too, had squatted for a closer look and was, to Leonard's relief, clearly intrigued.

"I just wouldn't get too close," Leonard said, and stood straight again, though there wasn't much about the thing that appeared particularly harmful. Still, he looked warily around the field, but everything was as still as still. Just the gentle nod of a few broad leaves from a breeze too light for either man to feel. Leonard heard the crow again, the buzz of some nearby bee, the whiz of a quick traveling fly and the two note call of a chickadee somewhere in the bordering woods. Then he heard the sudden rising zzzizzz of a cicada and anticipated that it would stop as abruptly as it had begun, but it didn't.

Leonard started to sweat. The smell of dead seaweed, the smell of salt too, grew stronger in a field that should have smelled of warm earth and cow manure and the green stuff of plants. And then there was that sound, as loud and intense as if the stupid bug that made it had fallen down the back of his shirt.

John stood up too, and poked the vine with the toe of his boot. "I don't know," he said, "Pretty weird. Can't say I've every seen a watermelon that anyone could flatten quite like that no matter what the size and shape of his butt." He fished a toothpick from his left front shirt pocket and put it in his mouth. First time Leonard had seen that. Maybe he thought it gave him the authority his young and handsome looks sometimes undermined. Who knew? But suddenly Leonard wanted a toothpick too. Something to do that might counteract a distinct sense of being swallowed by something, the sun, the sky, the harsh and endless neon sign buzz of that late summer insect.

"Gimme one of those," he said

John looked up, "What," he said.

"Those. The toothpick," Leonard said, feeling like he was shouting underwater.

"Yeah, sure," John said looking at Leonard now more closely while he brought his hand to his shirt pocket. "You okay?"

"It's just the cicadas," Leonard said. "Can't hardly hear myself think."

"Cicadas?" John said and listened, looking away, straining to hear. "Maybe one," he said looking back at Leonard and holding out a toothpick.

Leonard grabbed it and put it in his mouth, like he intended to crunch it right down and nearly did before he remembered what it was and what he'd wanted it for.

"So noisy," he said and restrained the urge to stick his fingers in his ears, but he knew it would not have done anything anyway - that the sound was coming from someplace more complicated than that. He wiped the sweat out of his eyes with the heel of his palm and sucked the toothpick like it was providing water to a man who hadn't had a drop in days.

"Now look at this. Look at this, John," Leonard said, "The one thing, the other thing I haven't shown you," and he squatted down again, to the plant next to the one he'd ruined. "See this?" he said and pointed to the gray-green vine that emerged from the leaves like a loosely coiled garden hose. Then he used his thumb to swipe the sweat from his eyes again. "Look close," he said.

So John squatted too, leaned forward and looked for a long time at the vine. Like most, it was covered with the tiny down of prickers, and the color was nothing unusual, like any that belonged to the melon or squash family. It looked hard, tough, though vulnerable he knew, to moisture rot, but there was something about it too, that reminded him of something else. A neck. That was it, like the neck of a swan or goose, or no, an ostrich except skinnier. Because under the prickly down, it looked kind of naked, kind of like skin, but translucent, a membrane of some kind that could have belonged to something that was a bird or a frog. And then he saw beneath it a movement as tiny as the pulse of an overtired eyelid muscle.

"See it? See it?" said Leonard. "What the hell is it, John?" he said, shouting over the zizzing zizzing buzz.

John couldn't resist; he touched it with his ring and middle finger, like he was placing them on the thin skin of a human wrist and found to his astonishment that it felt just as warm and soft.

He stood up fast and put his hands in his pockets. "That's some weird watermelon plant you've got there, Leonard," he said, and glanced around the field looking for what, he didn't know, finding that the quiet, the stillness, the field's resemblance to any other one in late summer, only made him more disconcerted, like whatever was in it had found itself a good disguise.

Nancy Bailey Miller

EDEN 1843

Abbie Alcott honored Bronson's schemes:
utopian farm, new home for their young brood,
until December came to freeze their dreams

of Eden. "Don't depend on cow nor teams
of horses for the plough, nor sheep for wool,"
said Bronson. Abbie honored all the schemes

while he went off to speak his vision. Means
for living from the land in summer could
beguile, until December froze those dreams.

Louisa May slept under attic beams
and played in orchards as her mother would
attempt to plant and honor Bronson's schemes.

Twenty shared the farmhouse, field and streams,
but Abbie dug latrines, prepared the food,
until December came to freeze their dreams.

The cupboard bare, the firewood gone, the reams
of books on tolerance—all in theory good,
mute on their shelves—she honored Bronson's schemes.
And still December came to freeze their dreams.

Hilary Holladay

THE HORSEMEN

My heart skipped within me thinking they had been Englishmen, ... but when they came near, there was a vast difference between the lovely faces of Christians, and the foul looks of those heathens. —*The Captivity and Restoration of Mrs. Mary Rowlandson* (1682)

They had finally crossed the Baquag,
thirty or so Englishmen in fine attire,
hats bobbing in sunlight, sashes flying,
radiant horses triumphing over the open field.
I clapped my hands, cried out praise to God.
Hope filled the space where hunger was;
if they were coming, then surely I was going
home.

Imagine, if you will, the rainy darkness,
the chill wind in my heart, when I saw them
for what they were, a company of Indians
dressed in English clothes. It was then
I looked down at my raw hands, my ragged sleeves,
and saw them in *me*: fellow impostor
tricked out like their starving
kin.

Some watery firmament caused us
to materialize in each other's eyes,
mirrored emissaries of God's encrypted plan.
It would take a captive more brilliant than I
to break the divine code of those noisome days;
to determine in a moment's glad, thundering arrival
which foul look to snub, which lovely face to
recognize.

Hilary Holladay

MANHATTAN BRIDGE LOOP, 1928

after the painting by Edward Hopper

It is quiet in Hopper's Manhattan,
impassive realm of wall and windowsill
that makes one almost overlook the man
below the sky. That restful sky can still
the nerves; the covering of light can soothe
a querulous heart. One's ear never hears
the grind of freight train or drone of uncouth
automobile—the art of engineers.
And yet that man who's almost left the scene
bears with him a steady, private sorrow
we recognize as if it could only mean
the very thing we dread, a subtle horror.
To watch him walk inexorably away
is to hear what one's own heart has to say.

The sonnet is based on the Edward Hopper painting owned by the Addison Gallery. "The Horsemen" comes from a book-length sequence, The Dreams of Mary Rowlandson, *recounting the adventures of the devout Puritan woman who was captured by Indians in 1676.*

Theodore Deppe

WIND WALK, CAPE CLEAR ISLAND

Back from a walk on the cliffs, telling Annie
how a pipit startled from the heather
and flew backwards a hundred yards in the gale
before settling behind frenzied gorse,

describing wave-covered seastacks,
how spray rose hundreds of feet and swept down harbor,
how rain on the rock path waterfalled uphill,
trying to tell her everything at once as I scramble

into dry clothes and Stravinsky's followed
on radio by the six o'clock news:
a Spanish trawler's sunk off Slyne Head in the storm
I've reveled in, the whole crew feared dead.

By morning, news of a different sort. In Cotter's Yard,
behind The Night Jar, dozens huddle in the rain,
tripoded telescopes trained on the hedgerow.
The crowd's silent until someone sees it again—

a bluewinged warbler, brought in by the storm.
It's the first time one has been seen in Ireland,
It's in the nettles I'm told, *below the montbretia,*
but I can't see it. The ferry runs non-stop,

bringing birdwatchers to Cape Clear—Father Peter
shakes his head and says, *If Jesus*
was sighted on the island, would so many
drop everything and travel here to see Him?

Years ago, I stopped the car near Mount Melleray
where a boy led pilgrims in the rosary.
It poured then, too, several women on their knees
in wet grass, the murmur of their prayers making

a music like the rain in the sally trees.
And the boy's sister, who'd also seen the Virgin,
was in hospital, trying to deal with what she'd heard.
I stared at Mary's statue. It did not speak.

One man has survived the trawler disaster.
Annie and I watch footage of his interview:
he looks up once at the cameras, then speaks
hoarsely to the white sheets of his hospital bed.

I have not seen the blue-winged warbler.
I don't know how many hundred birds perished
in the storm that brought him to this island.
I have not seen Mary move or heard her voice.

But Christ has a three day beard
and needs an interpreter. He cannot
rejoice in his own salvation. Grief or love
or rage prevents his looking at the cameras.

...if only hearts broke so beautifully...

~Brody Pagel

Anne Bradstreet

A LETTER TO HER HUSBAND,
Absent upon Public Employment

My head, my heart, mine eyes, my life, nay more,
My joy, my magazine, of earthly store,
If two be one, as surely thou and I,
How stayest thou there, whilst I at Ipswich lie?
So many steps, head from the heart to sever,
If but a neck, soon should we be together.
I, like the Earth this season, mourn in black,
My Sun is gone so far in's zodiac,
Whom whilst I 'joyed, nor storms, nor frost I felt,
His warmth such fridged colds did cause to melt.
My chilled limbs now numbed lie forlorn;
Return; return, sweet Sol, from Capricorn;
In this dead time, alas, what can I more
Than view those fruits which through thy heart I bore?
Which sweet contentment yield me for a space,
True living pictures of their father's face.
O strange effect! now thou art southward gone,
I weary grow the tedious day so long;
But when thou northward to me shalt return,
I wish my Sun may never set, but burn
Within the Cancer of my glowing breast,
The welcome house of him my dearest guest.
Where ever, ever stay, and go not thence,
Till nature's sad decree shall call thee hence;
Flesh of thy flesh, bone of thy bone,
I here, thou there, yet both but one.

Michael Cantor

WINTER CHILL

A cord of wood from Bartlett's Mill
spills on gravel; oak hits stone,
beech on pebbles; ash and birch
tumble down the ramp until
the cold air screams - the birds all flown -
and Bartlett's logs invent a church
which, rearranged with priestly care,
becomes an altar, stacked and square,
to fill the stove that blunts the chill
of damp Atlantic island night.
This salt-crust season of short light,
wind-blasted tides, white dunes bone bare,
demands that man and gods must share
the warmth that spares what winter tries to kill.

Michael Cantor

OCTOBER SPEAKS

(a poem for Boston)

It is ordained that things will fall apart.
Do not delude yourself – remember that
when summer ends I get to break your heart

with dark and practiced skill that makes an art
of pain, turns every champagne bubble flat.
It is ordained that things shall fall apart

again. You have no gods who can outsmart
a dead man's hex; no joyful *entrechat*
when summer ends. I always break your heart,

and yet you dance and hope for hope to start
each year, and dreams become your habitat:
it is ordained that things will break apart.

An ancient curse still plagues this land; its dart
contains the poison of a ruthless bat,
and summer's final ball will break your heart;

the wheels, bouncing, will come off the cart,
the true reliever shames the Theocrat:
it is ordained that things will fall apart.
When summer ends I get to break your heart.

Michael Cantor

HER LATEST GIRLFRIEND STOLE THE SILK TABRIZ AND LEFT BEHIND A CAT

And so, she lives apart, slim and austere,
among adobe walls of mauve and plum;
Tibetan prayer flags sway in cool dawn air,
their shadows skirl about her sleeping room.
She takes Ashtanga Yoga twice a week,
works at her job, brews pale green tea each night;
the Dalai Lama beams upon a desk
that sits between two bookshelves: her retreat.
And, now and then, she'll take a hike alone,
or ski, or see a film, or simply drive
at dusk through shades of hills and twisted pine
to watch the moon escape an ancient cliff:
and wonder why she needs to try again,
to be a judge of women, or of men.

Pamela St. Clair

LEFT OR RIGHT?

Since Friday, when Harold disappeared, Alice has been looking forward to this morning's walk. She's missed the flush of energy it adds to her day. Occasional twinges in her ankle remind her that it's still bruised. A horn honks twice, and she swears mildly beneath her breath—damn being as profane as she ever dares. She shades her eyes with her hand and turns to look, but the car has sped past. The commuter traffic rushes along in a blur of stock colors: blues, silvers, greens—the monotony of it all, every make and model painted from the same dull palette. No originality, she thinks, as a black SUV slaps a hot breeze in her face. Eyes on the ground, Alice silently talks her way to the corner, ticking off lists of chores: wipe down mirrors, thaw chicken for supper, sew button on her cardigan. Buy apples, Harold's prune juice, bread.

When she finally turns onto quiet Caleb's Road, she stops, as always, and takes a few deep breaths. So much has changed in the three weeks since she stumbled over a rock the size of a plump tomato and went down in a heap. How she managed to have the good fortune on that busy main road to fall on the grass she'll never know. And all those meddlesome people stopping to ask how she was. It was awful.

The weather has turned cool. She's glad she dug out her gloves. Colored leaves scatter across the ground. The fields to her left are variegated shades of spices: cardamom, paprika, nutmeg. She can almost smell them in the air. She should bake an apple pie. Perhaps have Ruth over. Ruth is always having Alice over, serving a honey-colored nightcap, which tastes, to Alice, like treacle. But Harold can't be counted on. Just last month he had wandered out in his underwear while the music club was practicing for its recital. Sally, who wouldn't know a whole note from a half note, has missed practices and been making excuses ever since. Of course,

Sally always hibernates when she and her current beau have had a spat. Alice has noticed a twin sheet, rather than a double, drying on Sally's line the past two weeks. Always looking for attention, that one. Well good riddance to those who can't even keep time.

Maybe Ruth is right. Maybe it is getting to be too much for her. But like Harold, Alice has never been good at making decisions. The two of them have managed to seesaw through life on an invisible fulcrum balancing this option and that, neither tipping one end higher than the other. Even their courtship extended for ten years. She had been almost thirty by the time Harold made up his mind.

In the past few months, Harold has taken to shutting himself up in the car. He sits motionless for hours watching their neighbors working in their gardens or heading to the community hall for bingo or a card game. Alice likes that about the community, the busyness of the place—plenty of activities and people to occupy her time. Oh she had balked when Robert first suggested housing for the elderly. "I don't like old people," she had complained.

"But, mom," he had said, ever the diplomat, "you are old."

What did he know? And the pull-string in the bathroom annoys her. It hangs there as if to remind her daily that she's feeble. If she's sitting on the toilet and has a heart attack she's supposed to yank on it for help and be found with her skirt around her ankles? That would be the day.

Sometimes Alice tries to remember what it was like those first few years of marriage. An indefinable space had always hovered between them, as if Harold had already rolled up the windows and locked the doors. And Alice, even in their most intimate moments, had felt as if she was the shadowy twin of the real Alice, the one fully engaged in life while she, the shadow self, hovered in the background taking notes, an understudy waiting for her big break. She wasn't terribly disappointed when she found herself childless at forty. Motherhood was never a role to which she aspired. And then Robert came along, and yes, she admits, she managed to adapt. And Robert's a good kid. At least he visits without an agenda. Sally's kids show up only when they want something. And

Ruth's daughter is always breaking her heart. How many illegitimate children now, three? four?

What, she wonders, does Harold think about in the car? When Robert was young, Harold insisted on Sunday drives. Alice would pack a bag of books and toys to keep Robert occupied in the back seat, and they would head out of town on what was then the only main route, until Harold felt like pulling off to wander along country roads. "Left or right?" Harold would ask at intersections. Alice would plan her responses in advance. If they passed any blue cars, her answer might be left. If not, right. If they passed a truck, left. If they passed two, right. Once Harold had caught her off guard. "Right," she had said, flustered, but then at the last moment, as Harold was about to turn, she changed her mind and yelled, "Left! I mean left!" The tires squealed as Harold yanked the wheel in the opposite direction, and Alice had laughed excitedly as she held the door handle to keep from sliding across the seat. They were soon careening around a wide bend too fast to brake for the mother raccoon waddling across the road with babies in tow. The thumps were sickening. Robert cried the whole way home.

Last Friday, she hadn't realized the car was gone until she went to call Harold for supper. "But why didn't the police call *me*?" Alice asked Robert when he called at two in the morning.

"They found my business card in Dad's wallet. They said he was driving like he was disoriented, so they pulled him over."

"Your father does everything like he's disoriented."

"It's late mom. I'll be by on Monday."

Krakau's farm hasn't changed in three weeks. Thin tongues of white paint have peeled away, exposing the dishwater-gray glands of wood beneath. Tattered curtains hang limply in the few upper windows not boarded up. The farm stands like a proud but shabby sentinel refusing to give up its watch. In its day, Krakau's grew the sweetest cucumbers. And she never tired of them—cucumber salad, cucumber sandwiches, cucumber soup.

A low stone wall edges the property. She had once seen a fox there, as still as the rocks on which it sat. Beautiful, really, with its glinting eyes framed by the red triangle of its face. She doesn't know a thing about foxes. Do they attack? Or are they more afraid of you than you are of them? She had been more worried about dogs. She doubts that in her hands a stick will be much of a weapon. But that fox! Alice believes in checks and balances. She has never owned any fur clothing, no fox stole or coat, so she had figured the universe would side with her on this one. But did it count if she didn't own one simply because she couldn't afford one? A steadily growing humming had made her look away to see a small plane skimming the fields. When she looked back, the fox had vanished. Where to with all that open land? Sometimes she wonders if she had really seen a fox at all.

At the end of the property, where the stone wall dwindles to nothing, Alice imagines it driven into the ground and continuing on the other side, winding through a labyrinth of underground fields and forests, where streets curve in slightly different directions and cars silently roll by in a spectrum of colors. And where her ankle doesn't throb. She stops, plucks out a bobby pin and tucks the stray hair blowing in her eye back into place. She'll have to stop at the farm today. No need to push her luck the length of her regular route.

"You're as old and creaky as I am," Alice says to the sign across the street. Faded black and red lettering announces, *Krakau's Cukes & Corn!* One post buckles slightly, as if bending backward at the knee. The faintest letters are the first and the last, as if the name is diminishing from the outside, in. The "u" is a gray ghost of its former self. Soon she'll be walking by *raka's* farm.

That's the word she couldn't think of this morning. Forty-four down: ruckus. With any luck, Harold will be dozing in front of the television, and she can finish her puzzle in peace.

***

"I don't think Dad knows who I am."

"Don't be silly," Alice tells her son. "Of course he does. He just doesn't like his program interrupted."

"What program? He's watching the local channel, a loop of town scenes shot in different seasons. And why isn't Dad eating at the table with us?"

"He eats in front of the t.v., or he won't eat at all."

"How's his appetite?"

"The same," Alice says, watching her son scrape pie remnants from his plate with the edge of his fork.

"The same as what?"

"The same as always. More pie?"

"I'll get it. Keep your foot up."

"Ruth's nightcap brew is in the cabinet over the stove."

"I'd rather drink anti-freeze. Has her daughter been by lately? What's her name? Lucy? Lacey?"

"Loose-y, all right. Her name's Libby. Why?"

"Just wondering."

"Just wondering, why?"

"Just wondering, because," Robert says, turning his back to her.

"When did you meet her?" Alice is positive *she* hadn't introduced them.

"Last spring, remember? One of her daughters pulled the emergency cord and the ambulance wail brought all of the walkers and canes to Ruth's door. She seemed nice, is all."

"Yes, well, she has three or four illegitimate children worth of niceness, is all." Alice is waiting for Robert to marry someone kind and normal, not that young girl he brought home with the pierced nose and *definitely* not the one who didn't believe in bras or shaved arm pits. She's learned not to ask. From where she is wedged between the back wall and the dining room table, the small alcove of a kitchen to her right and the living room in front of her, she contemplates Harold's profile, the narrow nose her son inherited, the square jaw he didn't, jowly now like a depleted balloon. He's examining the remote control, turning it in his hands, holding it out in front of him. Why had she picked all these somber shades of green? Old people green. She should have kept the paisley couch and those salmon armchairs. She turns and catches Robert licking the pie server. "When are you cutting off that ponytail?"

"When it doesn't bother you anymore," he says, walking over with the coffee pot in one hand and his pie in the other. "Dad, what are you doing?"

Harold bangs the remote on the coffee table. Alice has convinced him, no small feat, to wear the earplugs that came with the set so that she doesn't have to listen to it blare all day, and when Harold speaks, his voice hollers above the noise filtering in his ears. "God damn thing doesn't work!"

"Turn it around," Alice yells, tapping her spoon on her rim. She does this all the time, two or three taps after she stirs in sugar. Tap, tap, tap. "Turn it around. You're pointing it at yourself."

Bang, bang, bang. Robert takes four long strides into the living room and grabs the remote. "Dad, here, point the fat arrows at the t.v. Like this, see?" He hands the remote back to his father, who turns it over in his hands, examining it as if he's never seen it before. "Dad," Robert points at the congealing lamb chop and shriveled peas. "Are you done eating? Can I take your plate?"

Harold points the clicker at his son. "Who the hell are you?" he bellows.

Robert spins around, and Alice sighs. "Yes, he's done."

***

The convalescent home smells exactly as she imagined, antiseptic overlaid with something more difficult to pinpoint, like the stench whisked eggs leave behind in a metal bowl. It makes her ankle throb and her head ache.

The doctor had suggested they wait a few days before visiting so as not to confuse Harold. He hadn't made any fuss at all when they brought him here last week. In the car he had been positively calm, happy almost, humming under his breath, as Robert took the scenic route, driving around town for forty minutes before heading here. All the same, Alice feels as if they've tricked Harold, and she feels slightly queasy. They walk aimlessly up a corridor. It's all a maze to Alice, who suspects that, like her, Robert isn't in a rush to find his father. When she dares to peek in a door, the bareness of the rooms registers first, more a convalescent *ward* than a *home*. When they finally find Harold's room, it's empty. It looks as nondescript as all the others. She should bring in some things from home, maybe one of her knitted throws. A nurse, frumpy in that shapeless turquoise and pink smock get-up they call a uniform, suggests they check the common room.

Harold is sitting by himself in a row of chairs in front of the television. His sweater is on inside out, and his hair isn't combed, but he is shaved, Alice sees when she gets closer. The room is dim. Thin curtains are drawn across the only window high up on the left wall. Beneath it rocks a tall woman, hunched in the shoulders, her stringy hair pulled back in a purple bandana, her chin on her chest. Narrow blue veins map thin legs that disappear in the purple socks pooling at her ankles. Across the room, a man in a striped robe is strapped into a chair. His cropped head lolls to one side. Alice presses discreetly against the spot on her chest where sweat is gathering beneath her bra.

"Dad?" Robert stands in front of his father, but Harold waves him out of the way, craning around his son to watch some cooking show. A plump chef with ruddy trombone-player cheeks hops around the counter, banters with the audience, hops back behind the counter and tosses spices into a sizzling pan. The callisthenic cook, Alice thinks. She finds it tiring to watch him. She sits down on the other side of her husband. The seats are hard, little more than folding chairs. She is glad, for once, that a television is blaring. They learn how to make Cajun shrimp jumbo. Occasionally, Alice sneaks a peek at the other two people in the room. The man hasn't moved. Alice is ashamed at the urge she has to walk up to him and wiggle her fingers and poke her tongue out. She has read somewhere that the Queen's Guard outside

Buckingham Palace is trained not to flinch, regardless of any taunts from tourists. The woman in the corner rocks slowly back and forth, as steady as a metronome.

When the show ends, Robert leans forward to see around his father. "Mom, I have to get going soon."

Alice stands slowly. She hears her son, or she thinks she hears him above the television, asking Harold a question. If she places her weight just so on her heel, she can hobble with minimal pain. She'll have to take the van tomorrow. She certainly can't risk driving with her ankle feeling like this. Or maybe Ruth will bring her. "Harold?" Her own voice startles her. She's speaking loudly and slowly, as if to a child. "We have to go. I'll be by tomorrow."

"What?" Robert asks, leaning in toward his father.

"I want to go home," Harold says.

The doctor had warned her about this. "But this is your home," Alice says, hugging her pocketbook to her side. She is about to append "now," but thinks better of it.

"This. Is. Not. My. Home," Harold spits. His hands clench his knees. His bony knuckles are stiff and white.

"Dad?" Robert begins to squat in front of his father. "Would you like to go to your room, is that it?"

"Cock sucker!" Harold yells, and Robert pulls back quickly, the color draining from his face. Harold thumps his fist on the chair where Alice had been sitting. "Cock sucker!" he repeats over and over and louder and louder.

Where on earth? She has never heard Harold utter anything more shocking than her own limited lexicon of curses. Spittle has collected in the corners of Harold's mouth, and his face is as red as the callisthenic chef's. The room spins, and Alice takes everything in as if she's surveying it from the ceiling. She sees the top of Harold's head, the thin, stiff hair spiraling away from the bald spot at the crown, and his thumb, pressed tightly across the top of his fist, the nail turning scarlet, as he hits the chair. With a small shock, she notices her son's hairline receding farther away from the pencil thin slope of his nose. Neither the rocking woman nor the comatose man has flinched at Harold's outburst. His words sink through the television's din and crash in Alice's ears. She feels the full force of her body and stands rooted in astonishment, a sharp jolt shivering through her.

"Is everything okay in here?" a nurse asks, as she hustles into the room. Her flesh jiggles. White arms and face, pale and soft, remind Alice of kneaded dough.

"My father seems upset. He wants to go home," Robert says. Alice is afraid her son is going to faint. His tan skin has faded to the doughy color of the nurse's.

"Mr. Lydell," the nurse coos. "We talked about this, this morning. Remember?" When she bends over to talk with Harold, a thick gray braid falls over her shoulder. Alice thinks of the pull-cord at home in her bathroom, as if all Harold has to do is yank on that braid to save himself. "Would you like to go to your room? Are you tired?" When Harold doesn't answer she asks, "Perhaps a change of scenery? What about the game room?"

But Alice recognizes the glazed look that has coated Harold's eyes. He's gone, for the moment, staring blankly out of his own private windshield.

***

Since the two of them had developed the habit over the years of trying to stay out of each other's way, Alice had expected the place to expand in Harold's absence, but oddly, it seems to have diminished, instead. Maybe it's the green. Some bright pillows would liven things up.

Tomorrow night is the recital at the community center, and Ruth has insisted on coming over and doing Alice's hair, although Alice said she would be just as happy to pin it in her usual bun. "That's not festive!" Ruth had protested. *Festive* is one of Ruth's favorite adjectives. Have a piece of *festive* cake. Have you read this *festive* book? What a *festive* shade of lipstick! Alice wonders what Ruth will manage to find *festive* at the convalescent home.

"How's Robert?" Ruth asks. She's unrolling Alice's hair from around pink curlers. The tugs hurt now and then, and Alice is a little concerned that Ruth is finishing off her third nightcap.

Granted, Ruth is a good ten years younger, but Alice doesn't want to complain. This would cost forty dollars at the beauty salon.

"Oh, he's managing. Yesterday was difficult, what with Harold's outburst and all." She has told Ruth about it, but not exactly *what* Harold said.

"They say that happens to some," Ruth says. "Your vocabulary changes. Gets dirty. You heard about Doris, didn't you?" Alice shakes her head no, concentrating on keeping tears out of her eyes every time Ruth yanks. "She was over at Sally's just last week with the other members of the ladies' auxiliary. You know that silly bazaar Sally is so keen on organizing every year, even though it never makes any money? Well, they're sitting with their prim and proper tea and cookies when out of nowhere Doris says, "Oops, I spilled tea on my," Ruth lowers her voice, "pussy." Alice winces. "Sorry, did I pull too hard?" Ruth asks. Alice shakes her head no and waves her hand. "And then she just kept on blabbering about crocheting baby booties. Isn't that to beat the band? I bet those ladies practically fell out of Sally's plastic-covered chairs."

This makes Alice laugh. She can't imagine Doris, small 4'10'' Doris with her lopsided wig and her polyester pantsuit, saying such a thing. But she can imagine the ladies sliding around Sally's flower-splashed chair covers that squeak every time you so much as cross your legs.

"There!" Ruth says, brandishing a hand mirror. She has finished fluffing out Alice's hair and lacquering it stiff with hair spray. "Now don't move around too much in your sleep tonight. What do you think?"

Alice stares at the puff of cotton candy framing her puckered face. She's never gotten used to the lines around her lips and eyes and the shock white of her eyebrows. "Festive," she says.

When Ruth leaves, Alice cuts herself a wedge of pie for dinner. She brings it, along with a cup of coffee, to the dining room table. The caffeine will probably keep her up all night, but she feels depleted. She taps her spoon against her cup and wipes pie crumbs off her puzzle. She isn't getting anywhere with it. Late afternoon shadows spread across the room. "Crepuscular," she thinks, a word she learned from yesterday's puzzle. "I'm in my crepuscular years." Twilight sounds too flexible and promising, but crepuscular is onomatopoeic. It suggests her deteriorating, creaky body. The achy joints. The crustiness of old age. The damn sore ankle.

Harold's words thud in her memory. She can't bring herself to say them out loud, but silently she repeats the weighty sounds. Her head still tingles slightly. She stands up, tests her foot, and walks to the kitchen. She rinses off her plate, pours herself another cup of coffee, and reaches above the stove for Ruth's bottle. She pours a healthy dollop of the golden liquid into her coffee. Tomorrow she'll have to start sorting through Harold's things. Gingerly, she touches the shellacked curls, wondering how she'll ever sleep on them. In the window, her coiffed reflection stares back. The style doesn't look bad, really. She turns her head slightly to the left, then to the right. Across the courtyard, lights shine in a number of apartments. Green, salmon, plastic-covered, it doesn't matter. Inside, the room arrangements are identical. As the liquor reaches her bloodstream, warmth washes down the back of her head and spreads down her neck and shoulders. Superimposed over her own reflection, the twin lights from the tops of the town's water towers blink in the distance. Like fox eyes, small and mysterious, they flash at Alice across the night sky.

Lisa Harney

FERAL CLASH

Foxtail.
Flash of red, owned only
by embers
and phoenix feathers.

Attack is feline nature.
Claws like ice,
quiet ferocity.
It is not a drum beat
in my chest, but listen!
The thick, plush robes of a
gold-eyed monarch
matted with blood.

Oh, what to do when nature
Turns against you?
This rabid rage, this
foxtail.

Lisa Harney

AN APPEAL

Fluorescent lights beam
like headaches, and
we dare not rise from
our skeletal furniture.
I admit I jest
about these matters—
my geometric purgatory.
But the headaches
are no lie.

Eric Pellerin

THE PRAYER OF THE SMOKER

Dear God,

It is I.
A sub-human-
sneaking outside civilization to smoke a butt.
The December wind cuts my face,
as do the sharp glances of the passers-by,
passing judgment with their pretty, pink lungs,
ripe with self-righteous indignation,
having visited the oracle who told them:

You will live forever.

Wanna smoke with me, Lord?
I heard you hang with the lepers, beggars, and whores.
Wanna slum a bit further down the ladder?

Take one.
We'll breathe in together.

Place the Camels to our thirsty lips.

No filters
No lights
No ultra-lights
Low tar?
No tar?
No way!

Pussies, right God?

Quiet now.

Let's bring the matches to our lips.

Inhale.

Hold it, now.

Let Tobey and Nicky work their magic on our iron
lungs.

Hold it, now.

Breathe it all in.

I'll breathe in the endless piles of paperwork,
You breathe in the 100 years war.

Hold it, now.

I'll breathe in
the computer glitches,
the long rows of cubicles,
the pimple on my chin,
the copy due by five,
the coffee four hours cold,
the paper cut on my thumb,
the pain in my back,
the clinking of my car,
the kids screaming in my ear,
the wife's disapproving glare,
the eyes staring back at my reflection before I go to bed
wondering where it all went.
Hold it, now.

You breathe in
the gift of freewill,
the murders,
the rapes,
the poverty,
the racism,
the sexism,
the ageism,
the thisism,
the thatism,
the billions who died in your name,
the planet you created covered with hot top,
the blame you receive for all the above while

others walk away clean,
the sad sulks like me who take your list for granted and
rant about my own.

Hold it, now.

Together.

Breathe in oblivion.

Hold it, now.

Exhale.

Drop it.

Stamp it out.

Hold the door.

Eric Pellerin

ANYHOW

Is that my stillborn son in aisle 3?
feet falling free
from the cart pushed by
daddy
He wants something he can't grab
just out of reach
can hardly see it now
what was it
anyhow
rounding the corner
gone

Jennifer Feinberg

I'M SORRY

I knew she was there,
Alone on that table,
With the surgeons.
I wasn't allowed,
I had to wait.
I saw the video,
They taped it.
The line simply stopped,
So did my heart.
I knew she was there,
Alone on that table,
And I was watching TV.

Don Kimball

OUR FATHER

Our father fell this morning, broke his hip,
Leaving his flaws, while able-bodied sons
Kindly bore him through a Christian door,
Far from the house his father bought; this pater-
Familias, still holding, like a Pilgrim
Hymnal, that crossword puzzle he was snatching
From Mother's fingers, when he lost his balance;
Our father, now bedridden, fearing Hell –
"How she tried to lift him!" my sister cried;
As if, like Lazarus, a father could
Be resurrected; or Mother, like Mary M.,
Could be so bold and yet so meek, so old.
Our father, who's not yet in Heaven, fell
And left us all that fall on which to dwell.

Brenda Ayers Hajec

BLEEDING

My son's blood soaks the sheets
while the rubber-soled nurse runs
to get gloves. Red stripes spray across
her chest, the walls, the shiny tray,
like carnival spin art out of control.
I clamp my hand over the plastic tube,
the air sucked from my throat, my
vision dotted with tiny black spots.

The gurney shimmies as he twists
his wrist, pulling at the shunt, a wet ball
of adhesive tape filling his fist.
I tourniquet my body over his; I can feel
my shirt grow damp and sticky, a mixture
of his excess sweat and blood.
No one has read the chart tacked by his feet.

His clammy body convulses in the papoose
which held his screams for twenty minutes
as the needle slipped out of his vein,
pumping his life into the linen.

They all act like this. Soon, he will sleep.

The nurse lifts him off the vinyl.
Another hisses into the phone
What do we do now? His father wrestles
for our son's body, until he slips in the
widening puddle on the linoleum.
I watch as they both let go and drop him.

They will never get the blood out of the sheets.

Brenda Ayers Hajec

WAITING FOR THE THAW

— *for Cindy*

I'm sorry, we cannot bury her now.

How awkward it is to die in the wrong season,
to draw final breath in the middle of a snowfall.
And how hard it is for you, carrying home
the urn of ashes, children in the backseat
of the family wagon. The crying one
who thumps on the jar with her stocking foot.

In the spring there will be a service
and everyone will come and stand among
the flowers. Distant relatives.
New and sudden tears

as you and your brothers stand
stone-faced and still,
muted by the endless hours spent
packing away the tin measuring cups,
her small red diary, postcards from Germany.

Harry J. Durso

an excerpt from

THE T

I flagged over a tow truck that was at a traffic light, and he told me that my car was indeed condemned to the Tow Lot from hell. He remembered it because the radio was torn out of the dash, and he thought that the owner was so stupid to leave it overnight. I asked him for a ride and he laughed at me. The blue collars would win today. I was screwed, and I knew it.

The light changed, and the tow truck took off. The MBTA cop took a few seconds to write down the bus for me to take to the impound lot. "Take the T. You won't find a cab after a storm. The Green Line and the Red Line are down. Buses are running. You can walk from Andrews Square, if you want; but you'll never make it dressed like GQ, " he said as he smiled at a young beautiful doctor who looked like she liked him in some strange way. I waited for the stupid bus in my cashmere overcoat and Burberry scarf and Donna Karan messenger bag as the MBTA cop lined up his dates for the rest of the day shift.

The MBTA bus approached me covered with an array of snow, dirt, and gray dust that made it look like a great monster in the early morning light. I thought of Trinity one more time as if the thought of her alone would resurrect me from this self-imposed exile. The bus swallowed me up just as fast as I paid my fare and looked at a driver who loved his job almost as much as I loved my life. I looked for a seat that wasn't stained with the night before, and I sat down exhausted and looked out the incredibly dirty window. I called into my own office on the cell as if I thought someone was actually going to be there. "I'm going to be late," I said in one breath. No explanation needed because none was required. I was in hell as I thought I saw pieces of my BMW scattered on the ground. I tried to make myself fall asleep, as if I could again find peace in a bus that had traveled too many miles for its own good. I wanted to be alone, but I noticed that other lives were on the bus as well. I would not be alone.

I closed my eyes and opened them as some kid jumping on the bus screamed in my face for laughs. "Hey, bro, nice kicks, a lex on the wrist, a fag bag, and some fine bling bling. You are on the wrong bus, bro, but that's cool. It's all cool. ITS ALL COOL!!!!!!," he screamed, as he put on his disk player and then traveled instantly into space. I wondered if Trinity would take me back, and then I began to notice things around me as if I was a little kid taking the bus to Woolworth's with my mother. "Be careful of strangers," she would carefully say not knowing that I was condemned to live in a world of strangers. I pretended to sleep, but I was startled by my own loneliness. The bus made it to Andrews Square in its belabored manner, but I was becoming paralyzed with fear. I could not move. I gasped for my breath as the bus kept on moving and then I realized that some of the people around me lived on the bus. They never got off. I could not move as I realized that real live people would choose living on a moving bus rather than being in the real world. I saw a text message from Trinity on my new picture cell phone. " Go Away," she printed out. The only trouble was that I was going away faster than I expected.

The rhythm of the bus put me into a nervous sleep. I awoke to hear the woman behind me confessing into a toy cell phone. She confessed to telling the truth too much. She confessed to loving her husband too much and for showing too much consideration for a drug addled son who ultimately had her thrown out of her own apartment. She confessed to being afraid to run for her life. She confessed that she had too many dreams and that she was guilty of the crime of innocence. She asked God to forgive her for not turning to violence in enough time to save her own soul. She banged the phone on the back of my seat as she tried to coach an answer back.

"I'm sorry I was so good," she screamed and then looked out the blackened window as if she could see herself again. I looked at her and she smiled at me. She offered me a Hershey's kiss from a paper filled pocket and I took it and ate it as if it was holy communion. The bus moved on as I sat back down on my seat and saw my life pass in front of my now tear filled eyes.

A guy with a wool cap and a grease-stained NASCAR jacket got on and started to talk to. He told me that he just got out of prison and that he was going to sell his body to science one day because he was such a genius. He told me that the secret to life was to keep moving and to never let people know your real name. He tried to bum a butt off me and asked for a couple of bucks and that he would pay me back one day when our paths would cross so conveniently again. I gave him a twenty, and he jumped off the bus as if he was on fire fueled by the ability to buy a fix given to him by an innocent stranger too stupid to distinguish want from need.

I met a nurse who was going home after a double shift, and she told me about being in a ward where she saw so many miracles that she questioned when God said *no* and took one of her patients away. He would steal one from her when she wasn't looking.

I met a deformed man with a cane who told me he had a heart attack after finding his wife was unfaithful to him with a man young enough to be his son. I met a too young cleaning woman from one of the colleges who was smiling because she just found a fifty-dollar scratch ticket on the ground. I saw a little girl get on the bus with perfect cornrows, a bumblebee sticker on a test paper, and a smile as big as the sky. I saw a woman who read every word of the newspaper as if each word was a star in the heavens and a pregnant girl who held a doll in her hands as if it would stand by her.

I looked in my wallet and saw that I had had 900 cash and saw by the landmarks that the sun had set and that I might still have time to get my Beamer if I got off at the next stop and ended my exile. I got up and stuffed a hundred into the cell phone lady's hand. She held onto the bills and smiled as if I was part of a pleasant dream. I took off my Rolex and gave it to the cleaning lady. I gave my leather case to a college boy reading *No Exit*. I gave a gold pen to the man with the heart attack so that he had something to remember me by and then I was off the bus at Andrews Square. I skipped the cab and walked through the Big Dig construction sight maneuvering my way around its blasphemy; suddenly I saw my Beemer covered with snow, with a broken windshield, a missing tire and its convertible top ripped on one side. I ran inside the office and up to the barred window with its "Cash Only" sign, as the attendant, condemned to live his life in the misery of others, turned and shut the window. "Come back tomorrow," he said. I yelled and swore and cursed and was forgotten as quickly as I had forgotten to live my own life.

I went back out into a cold that only Boston in winter can have, and it took my breath away. I was going to make a call on my cell to a number of people who had no choice but to like me; but I, without hesitation, threw it down a hole that appeared out of nowhere. I saw the Beemer misshapen and deformed and lit by a buzzing cracked light overhead that spilled light over it like drizzle, and I started walking. I saw the Pine Street Inn and the Boston Herald, and I thought about taking my own life, but then I laughed for no reason. I climbed a chain link fence and headed to the expressway. I stuck my thumb out on the southbound lane knowing that I would be mistaken for a businessman whose car had died of potholes or a dead battery at an inopportune time. I would end up somewhere, I suppose. I only knew that the bus had taken me only so far. I had to travel the rest on my own.

Amale Chantiri Harb

VOICE AND MEMORY

His voice embracing
morning and evening...

an angry tune
echoed over the rooftops of the house
entertaining us as a lecturer
despising the silence.

his words pointed to the stars
fell down wisdom and love
over the rooftops of the house.

He, sometimes, gathered his tales
with all our childish eyes
as an avid collector,
fueled our dreams, tension and dream,
flowers and scents,
swords and shields,
games and fields
over the rooftops of the house, and
over our heads
a blessing from God.

His Thunder voice
made his ghosts shiver
our heart quiver
Suddenly, his wit spread, shredded
laughs, peace, smiles, and
in our soul, a prayer.

He wasn't a gypsy performer
or a cathedral lover
he was my father.

Paige Stevens

A MIXTURE OF LOVE AND LOSS

There really was nothing holding them together, no centrifugal force keeping them in orbit around themselves, and one might wonder why God had chosen to put them in a family unit in the first place, and furthermore, why they kept it that way. But a family they were, however dysfunctional. So we find them here, on a Thursday afternoon in winter, around a table. It so happens that the parents of this story are gazing, with some dissatisfaction, at the report card of their 15-year-old son who has slouched in his chair, fingering the dog collar about his neck. Their eighteen-year-old daughter is seated opposite the son, spoon feeding apple sauce into the mouth of her two-year-old.

The father of the family, Alden Lynch, is seated at the head of the table. His wife, Meryl, is seated to his right. Now it is often said of Meryl that she was the most beautiful woman ever gazed upon, and if this could be said of her, then the exact opposite could be said of her husband. While Meryl Lynch is tall and slender with gorgeous, long, cornsilk hair and clear azure eyes, her husband is both graying and balding, with more than a hint of a pot belly protruding out from the front of his business shirt.

The same beauty could be found in the features of their daughter Edie, who had inherited both her maother's hair and eyes. Their son Randell's looks ran more to his father's, although he already had slick, dyed-black hair and chains about his neck and was fully clothed in the same blackness that seemed to have permeated his personality. Seated on her mother's lap is the baby of the family, Edie's two-year-old daughter, Olivia, who holds the beauty of her maternal forebears in her toddler's face.

A car horn sounds outside the family's home, and while a look of reprieve flashes over Randell's face, Edie rushes around

the kitchen, swathing her and Olivia in layers of clothing to
protect them against the wet winter's night. The boy in the
pizza delivery car idling outside is Edie's boyfriend and Olivia's
father, Patrick. He taps the horn a few more times, and Randell
watches as expressions of disdain falls over his parents' faces.
Edie rushes out with Olivia into the dark night and Patrick
speeds off, snow flying from the curb under the car's wheels.

   "We'll speak about this again tomorrow Randell," his
father says as Randell clomped upstairs to bed. Alden and
Meryl disperse from the table, both clearing the dirty dishes as
they go into the kitchen.

*   *   *

   Their car ambled along the scenery of winter in New
England, headlights flashing past the pine trees, going
unnoticed, passing houses where Christmas lights blinked and
blue TV lights flashed from windows of quiet, sleeping houses.
Patrick reached over Olivia to stroke Edie's hair, and she glared
at him, her bright eyes flashing cornflower blue. Thursday was
their one family night together, where they usually ambled along
the country roads delivering pizzas to household families, then
driving to nowhere, usually not speaking two words to each
other, with Olivia seated between them. Sometimes they used to
go back to Patrick's apartment to have sex, but Edie stopped
that, fearing another pregnancy.

   "What's that for?" Patrick asked.

   "I just don't want you touching me anymore," she
answered.

   "Why's that?"

   "Because I know where it's always going to go. Last time
we touched, *this* is what happened," she said, gesturing towards
Olivia.

For a few moments they did not speak, just stared straight ahead out the windshield into the dark night. When they stopped for a red light in the deserted town square, Patrick leaned over across Olivia and kissed Edie square on the mouth. Edie fumed. "What the hell was that for?" she asked angrily.

"Will you marry me?" Patrick asked, still breathless and panting.

The first thing Edie was able to do was let out a sob, soon followed by wailing and rough, jagged cries. They didn't speak another word until Patrick drove them home, silently pulling up to the curb in front of the house where Edie stumbled out, clutching Olivia, falling on the icy walk twice. Patrick waited until they had both disappeared into the dark house, closing the door behind them. Then Patrick put the car in gear and drove off, leaving just a small squiggle of smoke in his wake.

When Olivia was put to sleep, Edie walked over to the Christmas tree with the multicolored lights that blinked on and off. She knelt down on the tree apron crunching pine needles under her weight. She picked up the baby Jesus, kissed it, and put it back in its cradle. She then picked up the Virgin Mary and thought how they had both been teenage mothers and she wondered if Mary had ever had the same feelings around her child, a mixture of love and loss of control. Maybe they didn't have the virgin part in common, but Edie felt a kind of kinship when she held the Virgin Mary. So much so that she took her upstairs to her bedroom and placed her on the dresser right under the light.

Judith Dickerman-Nelson

THE RIVER'S PULL

The river swallows drunken men
and small Cambodian brothers
but rats swim and the swift
current carries lighter things:
a styrofoam cup and a child's
broken doll bob along the surface.
a grocery carriage sticks out
from water, its criss-crossed metal
like a cage, like the fence
ripped back where the two boys
slipped through; curious, they felt
the river's pull…

maybe one held a stick
to watch the wake
created by its drag;
maybe an ancestor drowned
in the Mekong
and longed for company;
or maybe it was *jurng-gob*,
river monster lurking there.

Now a mother walks the edge
thinking she hears her children's cries.
It has been one hundred days
and she knows she'll meet
their spirits here. She brings rice
so her young boys won't go
hungry. She has heard them
calling in her dreams, seen
their round faces at the window
like full moons smiling, and now
she comes to greet their ghosts,
sprinkling grain to lead them home.

Rhina P. Espaillat

FOR MY GREAT-GREAT GRANDSON, THE SPACE PIONEER

You, What's-your-name, who down the byways of my blood
are hurtling toward the future, tell me if you've packed
the thousand flavors of the wind, the river's voice,
the tongues of moss and fern singing the earth.

And where have you left the rain? Careful: don't lose it,
nor the moan of the seagull in her blue desert,
nor those stars warm as caresses
you will not find again in your nights of steel.

Watch that you don't run short of butterflies;
learn the colors of the hours;
and here, in this little case of bones
I've left you the perfume of the seas.

Rhina P. Espaillat

PARA MI TATARANIETO
EL ASTROPIONERO

Tú, Fulanito, que por los caminos de mi sangre
te lanzas al futuro, dime si te llevas
los mil sabores del viento, la voz de río,
las lenguas de musgo y helecho que cantan la tierra.

¿Y dónde dejaste la lluvia? Que no se te pierda,
ni el gemir de la gaviota en su desierto azul,
ni esas estrellas tibias como caricias
que no encontrarás en tus noches de acero.

Fíjate que no te falten mariposas;
apréndete el color de las horas;
y toma, que en esta cajita de huesos
te dejo el perfume de los mares.

—from *Where Horizons Go*

Rhina P. Espaillat

SHELTER

How clever of my neighbor to devise
this little cage of nets in his front yard
to keep his children—and the toys they guard—
safe in the larger cage of Papa's eyes.

He's strung it between trees, by curtain hooks
from which four airy walls hang down: inside,
a wooden pony small enough to ride,
if you are small enough to read cloth books.

Light rain has grizzled the straw mane, and lends
weight to the text of flowery ABC's:
today rider and reader, on their knees,
are coloring indoors with noisy friends.

All of this bounded by the flimsiest fence;
its maker knows the stranger passing through,
armed with a knife, would know just what to do
to make a mockery of confidence.

And still my clever neighbor girds about
his irreplaceable--his priceless--things,
as if he knew some charm in sticks or strings
to keep the treasure in, the danger out.

(Margie)

Rhina P. Espaillat

BODY'S WEIGHT

"The soul is the heart
without the body's weight; mine joins the others
hovering like angels."
—"Notice," from <u>Ma and Other Poems</u>," by Morty
Sklar

But body's weight is all there is to link
one to another; who would know, without
that shared remembrance, when to turn and doubt
what the soul says to think?

I am afraid of those whose one desire
is unencumbered soul, those who believe
grace is a flair for lightness saints achieve
emerging from the fire.

Spare me soul's hard perfections; let the hands
of surgeons--lovers, too--learn to revere
and memorize what soul cannot hold dear
but body understands.

Let there be anaesthesia and fresh bread,
warm clothes in winter, and in summer, shade,
and let the saints forgive us what we weighed
as we forgive our dead.

(The Dark Horse)

Brittany Wadbrook

SEASIDE SCARS

A Villanelle

They cover themselves
Sunblock to keep out the unwanted
Sun rays, sting rays, always
Things to be careful of, very careful
They say a beach is a play to enjoy
Hell, they say a lot of things

She makes a lunch of healthy things
The kids are too young to make it themselves
And joey says mommy can we bring ted?
A Yes joey gets from under skin sunblocked always
From behind shaded eyes, a be careful;
A Yes, a be careful, an Enjoy

Criterion to them is telling us to enjoy
But it gets washed up with all other things
A real concern lies with an image of themselves
One that portrays a concern for ted
ted must be wearing sunscreen always
As with her image, he should be careful

Young minds are never careful
But they must let the boys enjoy
The sand crabs and old scabs, never could get rid of those
damn things
Scabs on each other, scabs on themselves
For just one moment, it's about Ted

Awkward, it's been about themselves always
ted watches the tide; it goes this ways and that ways
Of the undertow he must be careful
Not to be scabbed by what he enjoys
It's not their kids doing such foolish things
It's not themselves
Its not ted

It is Ted
He defies the rules always
Ted doesn't have to be careful
He can do all the things he enjoys
But Ted is washed over by the enjoyable things
For just one moment, it's not about themselves

About themselves they've faked a concern.
Always careful to appear to enjoy taints precious things
Ted will not enjoy drowning.

Brittany Wadbrook

MODERN PASTORAL

They lassoed lightening to her eyes
And painted sundrops to her skin
Shaved space from the inner thighs
Hemmed her waist with a conceited pin

They let fireworks manifest in her smile
And gave life to fried strands
They trimmed the faults of her profile
And let dew drops make home in her hands

Glazed-over oculi still let us connect
To living things below dead skin
An honesty hidden by pretend perfect
Prohibits the real deal material within

They gave her a milk glass half full
And slapped her on a poster
But he told her, under, she was beautiful
Every goddamn dead cell on her.

Brittany Wadbrook

THE TEMPEST

It's overcast that's masking
The glitter in your pupils
How unfortunate the riptides
That pull corners from your lips
And the waves rolling over threads of your skin
Ironed onto the bones that creak when they sway
It's between the arched brows that quiver nervously
Against the gush of liquid covering her coating
A moment wedged within
The cascades rushing over ironed sheets
That crease around her binoculars
Binoculars that hunt the room
For the exact heat exchange
        Between the upper and
                Lower atmosphere
The occluded front collision
That caused
This storm.

Meg Sullivan

LOST AND FOUND

Sean was kneeling on the living room window seat with his nose pressed up against the glass, his chin cupped on both hands. A silver car went by on the street outside and his eyes widened with anticipation, but it failed to turn into his driveway to produce the stout frame of his father. After a few false hopes, his breath had fogged up the pane before him, and he distracted himself by drawing a little picture of a ghost in the condensation.

"Sean, please don't smudge the windows, OK?" his mother's voice wafted from the kitchen. "I just cleaned them this morning."

She was like a hawk. Sean glared over his shoulder while he wiped the glass clean with his sleeve, then returned to his vigil. He bet that every other six-year-old in the world was playing outside in the sun right now, laughing and running and getting dirty while he was stuck waiting in his neat, stuffy house. The tie his mother had secured tightly under his collar made his neck sweat.

"Maa, can't we go wait in the park?" Sean whined, his words clouding up the window again. She didn't respond, but just sighed deeply and mournfully. He turned around to watch his mother's back as she pretended to straighten their spotless kitchen. His shoulders swayed back and forth as she rearranged the salt and pepper shakers. First they moved next to the breadbox, then over by the stove, then next to the spices and back again.

"Mom!" Sean yelled, letting the frustration spill out into his voice. Her head slowly turned to look at him, but instead of looking irked, she had an expression of exhausted sadness on her face. Sean scowled.

She spoke softly. "Just hang tight until Daddy gets home. He'll be here soon, and then we'll head out, all right?"

Sean jutted out his lower lip and crossed his arms. "Soon" had long been over, and he was sick of waiting. He pounced on the weariness in her voice.

"Well, I'm going to the park," Sean announced, hopping off the window seat with a 'humph.' He made sure he stomped his feet extra loud as he walked towards the door, making sharp echoes reverberate through the house. "You don't have to come. I'll just go to Dezzy's house and get *him* to go with me instead."

The Hendersons lived two houses down the street and their son Dezzy had always been known affectionately by the neighborhood as a 'blond firecracker.' Dez had been Sean's best friend ever since they met in preschool three years ago. The two of them built a block rocket ship on the first day of school, flew to the edge of the universe and back, and had been inseparable ever since.

His mother's chin snapped up and she gazed at Sean, her eyes loaded with worry. "Sean, please," she whispered, twirling her wedding band anxiously. She paused and seemed to search Sean's eyes for a moment, then shook her head slightly and signed again. In a firmer voice, she went on, "You're too young to be crossing the street by yourself, and I don't want you mussing up your dress clothes."

Sean didn't respond and started to open the door, keeping his eyes locked with his mother's in a challenging stare. A warm autumn breeze carried the noise of traffic through the doorway, and Mrs. Coolidge cast a worried glance to the busy street outside. Sean watched the resolve in her frame crumble, and smiled with relief as she gathered her hat and sunglasses and left a note for his father. He held her hand tightly as they crossed the street to the park.

*   *   *

"Now remember: I don't want you getting dirty, so no slides, no puddles, and no sandbox," Sean's mother warned him as she arranged herself to wait on one of the park benches. "As soon as Daddy gets back from the office, we're leaving. No complaints, all right?"

"Ya, sure, Ma," Sean said absentmindedly, craning his neck to look for Dezzy. He thought he saw a blond head next to the tire swings, and as soon as his mom was done with her lecture, Sean scampered off calling his friend's name.

By the time he reached the swings, they were pathetically empty. No Dezzy. Sean scowled with disappointment and cast another glance back to look at him mom. She was slumped into the park bench with her straw hat tugged low over her eyes, absorbing herself in watching him. The playground before her was ringing with the hum of bees and children's voices, but she seemed to remain deaf to it all, caught up in a separate world.

Sean could tell she was upset again by the way that she was picking at the fabric of her skirt. Her slender fingers pulled the folds in the dark cloth as if she were plucking petals, and the fabric was beginning to stretch from the constant tugging. He could always tell how distressed his mother was by the amount of worry wrinkles in her clothes.

Sean sat on one of the tire swings and twirled around, pushing off with the toes of his new oxfords. His mother swayed in and out of his line of vision. On his third twirl, he saw a flash of red darting past the monkey bars.

"Dezzy! Hey, Dez!" Sean yelled, leaping off the tire and waving his arms. His friend didn't come out, but Sean knew where he was hiding now and ran over to join him under the slide.

"Sean, be careful of your dress pants!" called Mrs. Coolidge from across the playground. Under the slide, Sean rolled his eyes at his friend. He cast an exasperated glance towards his mother. She had her darkest sunglasses on, and her hat was pulled so low that it almost covered her eyes. Although her face was calm and sensible as she gazed towards them, her hands were fretting up a storm. Sean wondered why his mom was so upset lately.

Last night at dinner she had plucked at her blouse all through the lasagna and into the apple crisp. She had been watching him then too, so intensely that the weight of her eyes made the fork in his hand shake. Later in the evening, she had insisted on tucking him in under his Superman blanket and kissing him goodnight, something that Sean had protested against vigorously since his fifth birthday. He had grimaced and allowed it only because of whorls of crinkles that covered the hem of her shirt.

In the morning Sean had examined his mother's outfit as he sat at the table waiting for blueberry pancakes. The cloth was smooth and unmolested, but as soon as he mentioned wanting to invite Dezzy over to play, her face lost its cheer and her hands lunged for the edge of her blouse.

His mother's face had creased itself in worry wrinkles as she started to say something, but her voice cracked and she looked away. As Sean ate, she dialed his father at the office with one hand while worrying her cotton sleeve between the fingers of the other. Sean couldn't tell what she was hissing over the phone, but he could tell that they were discussing him by the way his mother kept eyeing him over her shoulder.

"So what do you wanna play today, Dez?" Sean asked, turning to his left and putting thoughts of this morning out of his head. His best friend was sitting cross-legged with his favorite Spiderman t-shirt on, the dark shadows of the slide making his face hard to see.

Dezzy shifted in the grass and tossed around a few pebbles, pretending to think about it, even though they both knew what he would say. Suddenly he let out his trademark howl, an ear-splitting mix between a wolf and Tarzan, and beckoned Sean out into the light. The sun reflecting off the playground was so bright that Sean could only see by shading his eyes and squinting, but he could hear every word Dezzy said clearly. "Let's go look for the lost treasure of Atlantis!" Dez exclaimed. Sean rolled his eyes and moaned.

"We always play that game," he complained, "and we've never even found the treasure!"

"Well, that was when we were just pretending," Dezzy said matter-of-factly. "That was practice. This time it's real. Real sea monsters, real treasure and everything."

"Sea monsters?" Sean asked, peering at Dez nervously.

"Yaaa," Dez whispered, leaning in close. "They've got six tentacles and seven eyes and teeth the size of your arm! They would be the scariest thing you'd ever laid your eyes on, except for..." He paused.

"Except for what?" Sean asked, not really wanting to know, but feeling obliged to ask.

"Except they're invisible!" Dezzy hissed, excited with his own genius. "They're the deadliest creatures on earth, and you don't even know where they are, until SNAP!" He clapped his hands loudly, causing Sean to jump back an inch. "They bite a chunk out of your leg! And then you're nothing but fish food."

Sean's eyes began darting to the grass at his feet, and he looked progressively more and more nervous. "I don't think I wanna play that game," he whispered without conviction. "Let's do something else, Dez, OK?"

"Why? You aren't *scared* are you?" Dezzy smirked as he teasingly skipped through the monster-infested grass.

"I'm not scared!" Sean snapped automatically, eyes glued to Dez's feet.

"Well then, let's play. First one to the ship gets to be captain!" Dezzy yelled, darting off towards the seesaw.

"Sean's eyes widened and he hesitated a little before he ran off as well, calling, "Dezzy, wait! Where are the monsters?"

His friend didn't stop, and Sean sprinted to catch up. Suddenly Dez started running in huge zigzags. "There's one!" he yelled, dodging to the left. "And one over there!"

Sean shrieked and jumped over the invisible menace. A girl in overalls and pigtails looked quizzically at him.

"Sea monsters! Everywhere!" Sean called out to her. The girl shook her head and returned to her toy horses.

The two boys leapt and fell and ran, dodging monsters so often that, within a few minutes, they were no closer to their ship than when they had started. Suddenly Dezzy squawked as a group of invisible creatures pounced out from under a bush. He zigged as Sean zagged. While Sean clambered to the top of the jungle gym, Dez leapt between the swings and over the sandbox. Suddenly he screeched to a halt.

"Sean, help! I'm surrounded!" he cried out.

From his safe perch, Sean's heart dropped and landed on his stomach. He felt sick. Dezzy was out there all alone, and Sean was scared that if he jumped back on the ground, a jaw full of two-foot teeth would bite his leg off. He didn't know what to do.

"Dezzy, I don't wanna play anymore!" he wailed mournfully.

"I told you this isn't pretend. You gotta help me! Please, Sean!" Dezzy yelled, sounding truly distraught. "I can feel them circling me!" He kicked out his foot at the air on his right, trying to ward off the monsters.

Sean was beginning to panic, and his mind whirred in hopeless circles. Finally he just held his breath and jumped from the safety of the metal bars, praying that he wouldn't land in the gaping maw of a sea beast. He couldn't lose his best friend.

"I'm coming, Dezzy!" Sean called as ran. He pumped his slender arms as hard as he could and tried to make his legs blur with speed, like they did in the cartoons. When he glanced down, though, they were still normal legs running at a normal speed in his black pants and oxfords. No blur.

Dezzy shrieked, and Sean ran faster, shivering as he felt something brush up against his leg. He was beginning to gasp out of breath, and Dezzy was still so far away. Sean felt despair beginning to creep in.

"I'm Superman. I'm Superman," he panted to himself, trying to ward off thoughts of failure. If Superman were bulletproof, he was surely also sea monster proof, and super heroes would never give up trying to rescue a friend. Sean just closed his eyes tight and sprinted forever. The world got louder, filling his ears with the sound of his own laboring lungs and Dezzy's squeals. The ground pounded beneath his feet and sea monsters snapped their jaws, but Sean kept on running. Just as he began to think that he would collapse and Dez would be lost forever, he opened his eyes to find his friend right there beside him. Somehow he had scraped through the jaws of death untouched.

"You saved me, Sean!" Dezzy said with a fierce smile. "Quick, let's get out of here." Sean nodded, ready for anything. Together they took a deep breath and howled their most horrible howls, momentarily confusing their predators with the noise. They leapt away from the invisible killers and scrambled to the safety of their seesaw ship, leaping atop the metal support. The two boys clung there, hugging their knees and catching their breath, silently stunned at the dangerous turn their games had taken.

Hesitantly, Sean spoke up first. "Maybe there shouldn't be sea monsters anymore, Dez."

"Yeah," Dezzy whispered, looking over at Sean timidly. "I think they decided to move to Antarctica or something. I hear they like the cold water."

Sean nodded his head in relief. He paused for a moment, then said, "No more dangerous stuff, OK?"

"'Kay, I promise."

Sean squinted into the sun and saw Dez nodding his head firmly. He breathed a sigh of relief. They silently agreed to sit there a little while longer, allowing time for any straggling sea monsters to leave the park and get on their way to Antarctica.

Sean once again turned to look at the park bench and saw his mother watching him with another frown on her face. He didn't understand why her brow was so often etched with worry lines lately, or why she was acting so strangely. Sean remembered that last night when he brought Dez home for dinner, she hadn't even acknowledged him. She refused to set him a plate for dinner, which set Sean off on a temper tantrum. Dezzy seemed not to mind. Sean ate his dinner as Dezzy ran around his house, shooting webs and pretending to be Spiderman. He figured that Dez was probably allergic to lasagna and apple crisp. Sean finished his meal quickly and refused to respond when his mother tried to talk to him, ignoring her concerned gaze, watching Dez instead. After he ate, Sean ran off to play super heroes with his friend. His mother remained at the table and sipped at her coffee with a troubled expression.

Sean took his eyes off the dark shape on the park bench and returned his concentration to willing away every single monster from the park. Surely all the beasts had to have left by now. After ten breaths, he nodded to Dez and they both hopped to the ground at the same time, trying not to wince as their feet came within biting distance. Standing safely in the grass, Sean let out a deep sigh of relief.

"Let's go find that treasure."

*   *   *

With the help of a couple of local sea horses, Sean and Dezzy learned the exact locations of the lost treasure of Atlantis. The sea horses dropped them off at the sandbox over by the monkey bars, and as they stood over the soon-to-be discovered treasure, the two boys looked at each other. Sean's eyebrows were quivering as if he were holding them back from exclamation, and the corner of Dezzy's mouth twitched. They laughed, a little louder than usual, as if to tell the invisible beasts of the world they there were no longer afraid. Then Sean pounced into the sand to start digging with gusto. Soon sand was flying everywhere.

"How deep do you think they buried it, Dez?"

"Just a little deeper. I bet we're almost there."

"Do you think there'll be a lot of pirate gold?"

"A whole treasure chest full!" Dezzy breathed, digging faster.

"With jewels?" Sean asked, poking at the sand with a stick.

"Rubies the size of your head!"

The two friends grinned together, and Sean continued to throw sand around the sandbox, the treasure growing in his imagination.

A shadow fell over Sean's shoulder, and he looked up into the sun to see his mother standing above him. She had taken off her sunglasses to look at him, and her eyes were dark and endless.

"Sean, what did I tell you about going in the sandbox?" she asked harshly with a disappointed glower. "Now look at you! You're covered in sand!"

Sean's mouth fell open. He had completely forgotten about his mother's mandate. Looking down, he saw the sand crusting the wrinkles of his outfit.

"I'm real sorry, Ma. I forgot," he said, biting his lip and looking up at her with his best doe-eyed expression. He added a little sniff for good measure.

His mother sighed and softened her voice. "Well, your father is here anyway, so it's time to go," she said, reaching out her hand for him to take.

Sean eyed her outstretched arm, but didn't take it. "But Ma, we're looking for the treasure of Atlantis," he said hesitantly. "Can't we just go after we find it? We're gonna be rich!"

Mrs. Coolidge flinched. She glanced around the turmoil of the sandbox as if looking for someone, seeming as if she didn't know what to say. After a pause and a deep breath, she said, "Well the treasure will just have to wait 'til tomorrow, OK?" We have to go now, or we'll be late." She helped Sean out of the sandbox and brushed off his pants and jacket. As she turned to lead him back to his father and the car, Sean dug in his heels.

"Wait, Mom! What about Dezzy?" He tilted up his chin, looking innocent and confused. Mrs. Coolidge breathed in sharply and knitted her eyebrows together with concern.

"Oh honey," she whispered, kneeling down to envelope her son in her embrace. Sean squirmed a little, then held still. His mother tenderly smoothed his sandy hair for a moment then kneeled back and looked him in the eyes. "I know it's been really hard for you this past week, Sean, but you have to accept that Dezzy's gone." Her voice broke, and she wiped some moisture from her eyes. "He can't come back. He's gone. You have to understand, baby."

Sean pulled away from his mother violently, starting to cry as well and angry with himself for it. "No, Ma! Dez is helping me look for the treasure. He's right over…" Sean turned around, past the empty sandbox, looking wildly for his friend. "He's right…I bet he's right behind that tree. I know it; he's hiding, Ma! Come on. We'll go get him and he can come with us!" Sean's eyes were pleading and desperate as he tugged at his mother's skirt. His pointed little chin quivered.

Mrs. Coolidge didn't move from her kneeling position, and a tear fell from the corner of her eye. "He's gone, honey. If I could bring him back, I swear I would do it in an instant, but we just can't, Sean."

"No, no, no, no!" Sean mumbled, "It's not fair!" Salty droplets made tracks on his dirt-stained face as he shook his head and pushed against his mother's restraining arms. His voice got louder and more vehement. "No!"

"Sean, please," his mother whispered. But he would not listen. He was trying to block out her words, block out those thoughts. Dezzy Henderson was right behind that elm tree, he knew it.

"Dezzy!" Sean yelled, "Dez, you can come out now!" His mother picked him up and started carrying him towards his father and the car. "Dezzy!" He screamed, kicking at the air and clawing at his mother's arms. "Dezzy, come on!" He wailed his friend's name over and over, but Dezzy stayed behind the tree. The car door slammed shut, and Sean plastered his face to the window, fogging up the glass with his tearful yells.

*   *   *

By the time they arrived at the wake, Sean's sobbing had diminished to a weak sniffle. He sat huddled in the back seat, clutching the seat belt to his chest as if it were a life preserver. Sean didn't speak and showed no sign of noticing that the car had stopped moving. He kept his eyes glued to the window, still watching that elm tree, still waiting for Dezzy to come back out. Mrs. Coolidge opened the side door and gently disentangled him from the nylon strap. She wiped a little of the dirt and salt from his cheeks, then clasped one of his clenched hands in hers and walked with him and his father into the funeral home.

Sean followed his parents into the world of black. It was as if a huge fire had passed through and left everything coated in ash. Practically all he could see were legs and feet. Black pants with black shined shoes, black skirts with black heels, and at least three pairs of legs wearing the same pants and oxfords that he was wearing. Sean was horrified to see how well he blended in with this place and these people that he had never met, and he was afraid that if he closed his eyes he would blend in and lose himself. Sean clutched his parents' hands more tightly to make sure they didn't leave his side.

As they brushed past groups of murmuring dark figures, Sean became acutely aware of the sand that still clung to his shoes and lines his pockets. He tried to make himself look smaller as they progressed through the black maze, hoping no one would notice him.

Mrs. Henderson stood at the front of the room beside a polished wooden box looking stiff, blanched, and awkward with the cast on her arm. The anguish on her face seemed familiar to Sean, as if the passing of his friend's life were written there in the crease of her brow.

Mrs. Coolidge brought Sean right up next to Dezzy, so close that he could hear every word of the priest's murmured prayers. He looked down at his friend, expecting to see the mad grin and Spiderman t-shirt but found neither. Denzel Henderson lay in his small coffin with an expression of calm innocence, dressed in a suit and tie similar to Sean's own. Sean's heart leapt to his throat and his breathing became ragged. Images of his best friend flashed before his eyes: Dez laughing, eating spaghetti with tomato sauce all over his cheeks. Dez climbing a tree, throwing a stone at a flock of geese, whirling around in Sean's yard until he fell from dizziness. And all they added up to was this: a motionless doll that had stolen Dez's face and wore it in a box. Sean wanted to yell at him to get up, to come back to the park and play, but he held his tongue bitterly. It didn't seem right at all, and he clung behind his mother's skirt to hide the warm rush of tears.

In silence, Sean's father paid his respects then gently ruffled his son's hair before he went over to murmur with a crowd of pants. The mother and son stood by the coffin for a long moment. Occasionally an adult or two would glide by to murmur condolences to the Hendersons, pausing to look back and forth between the two young boys in similar suits, one crying and one eternally calm.

Sean was in a daze. He couldn't accept that this would be the last time he saw his friend, that Dezzy was actually gone. Dez was lying there right in front of him, and all he had to do was open his eyes and everything would be all right. Sean stared at the box. He could hear snippets of the whispered conversations around him, and tried to fill his head with words to cover the pain. Inconsequential babble about the weather, pets and lilies washed over his conscience, calming him and allowing him to try and forget. But then Sean heard his father say words that made his heart want to explode.

"Drunk driver," he said. A murmur and a sigh. "No, still no leads. It's just a shame." Sighs of agreement, a sniffle.

Sean's parents sat him down the night it happened, trying to explain. He'd tried not to hear. He didn't believe them. It just couldn't have happened. Dezzy had taken his seat belt off for just a moment, reaching for the Spiderman action figure that had fallen under the seat. Just one moment and the word had snapped him up in its jaws. Sean had known it couldn't be true, but he looked down at his friend, and everything his parents had said rang in his ears tauntingly. He hugged his mother's legs, trying to hide the coffin from his vision.

Eventually, after Mr. Henderson led his wife to a chair to sit in a dazed silence, Sean's mother began to gently guide her son away, but Sean resisted. He still didn't feel right, like there was something incomplete. He racked his mind for a moment and remembered the sand that lined his pockets. Sean disengaged himself from the folds of his mother's wrinkled skirt and approached the coffin. Glancing to make sure the priest wasn't looking, Sean reached into his pocket for a pinch of sand from the site of the treasure of Atlantis, and sprinkled it over Dezzy's clasped hands.

As he tread away on his mother's heels, Sean gave one last glance over his shoulder towards the polished wooden box. Dezzy was standing there next to the huge treasure chest with his mad grin, wearing his favorite Spiderman t-shirt and light-up sneakers. He waved, and Sean waved back. "Bye, Dezzy," Sean whispered.

Helena Minton

CODA

In memory of my father

You used to say it ran in families,
this sense of time.
Your wristwatch glinting
beneath a crisp cuff,
you set the standard,
but it wasn't a strictness
you instilled, more of a personal attribute,
like the way we smile
or move our hands when we talk.
It makes us feel better to be on time.

From the moment I heard you were sick
I fell behind.
They were already sweeping
your hospital room,
preparing your bed
for someone else,
when I arrived.

I thought I'd be at loose ends
yet even months later
I feel I will never catch up.
What I'm racing towards
is not the ocean liner
pulling away in a dream

but minutiae,
chores and purchases,
three calendars I mark
and forget to double check,
bills, letters, phone calls.

Why is it so satisfying
to cross out *milk*
and *dry cleaning*,
to gun my way
to the next errand?

I've forgotten what it's like
not to know what to do next.
Grief has become a bureaucracy.
I go through channels
to reach you.
In line I clutch my lists,
thinking of you,
your congeniality, your wit,
your traits become
small things written down.

Helena Minton

THE BIRCH

The week before my wedding
how did we find a moment,
my father and I, who rarely
worked together with our hands?
It felt urgent that we dig,
heft the compact root ball,
lower it, pack in the dirt.
Less urgent as we stood back
and admired what we'd planted,
the white trunk with fringed leaves
a head taller than the ring bearer.
Underfoot, myrtle spread
its intangible blue flowers.

Rich Farrell

THE BOGEYMAN

I still have nightmares about the day me and Artie Fossett were at the old YMCA lifting weights. The day Tommy Parks pranced into the room, grabbed a forty-pound weight, threw it against the wall, and announced to everybody that he was gonna kill me for taking Patty Kelly away from him.

Tommy was a crazy mother with quick hands and maniac strength. But I wasn't scared of nothing back then. And besides, I wasn't about to give up my French-kissing sessions with Patty every night at the Shed Park Field House.

I remember, Tommy's quick blue eyes were wide and violent. And for an instant, I almost blurted out a lie. I liked to lie back then. I wanted to tell Tommy that me and Patty had done all the bases and we were rounding third for home. But you know, somehow, no matter how much I wanted to say it, something told me to shut up.

"Meet me at Shed Park in an hour," Tommy challenged. "I'm gonna teach you a lesson about touching people's property."

"I'll be there, pimple nose," I said real brave like.

What could I say? It was a matter of pride. Everybody would have called me a coward. What would Patty have said if I hadn't defended her honor and stood up to her ex-boyfriend? Besides, Tommy was such a fake.

Okay, well I spent the next half-hour finishing my workout. No way was I gonna let anybody know I was scared, never mind even thinking about it. So I kept my best poker face until Artie spoke up and my stomach started with the somersaults.

"Nervous, Jake?"

"Nah!"

"Well, we better finish up if we're gonna make Shed Park! You know—we don't have to go."

"What you talkin' about?"

Artie was my best friend. He wasn't a fake at all. He lived right next-door, short, cute, little squirt with a dimple in the middle of his chin. All the girls loved him. But you know how best friends are—they always say what you're thinking.

"We'll, you know, Tommy is one tough kid! I've seen him kick ass. Mean it. These two kids from Tewksbury gave him a rash of bull one night at the drive-in. God; he booted the crap outta both of them. They were much bigger than him too, Jake!"

Now, why did Artie have to tell me that. I was a little scared before, well you know only natural, thinking about what would happen to my position in society if I lost and all.

"Yeah, well, we'll see," I said. "I'll kill him."

I remember looking at the clock in the YMCA lobby; I had fifteen minutes to get there, no car, and nobody to bum a ride from. We'd never make it by foot. And that's when Artie suggested we thumb. He said we'd get one ride and be there in five minutes.

But that wasn't true. This hippie-kid gave us a ride almost all the way. I tried to talk him into going just another mile. Told him I had to be there early. Told him how important it was to have time to psyche myself up. But he was high on some ragweed and just laughed.

We couldn't run the distance because I'd be out of gas. Tommy would surely have killed me then. So, what did I do but stick out my thumb one more time. And you know, if I wasn't so desperate, I would have seen Dad coming. I always watched for him.

"Jesus H. Christ!" Dad's voice appeared like vapor in thin-air.

Artie ran. Before I even opened the door handle, his back was nothing more than a blur.

"Dad, let's talk about it."

"Sure, we'll talk about it. Get in. Right now!"

Somehow, I knew the moment my ass hit the seat that most of the talking would be from his mouth, not mine.

Whack. Whack. Whack. Open hands bounced off the side of my face. My eyes filled from a quick shot to the bridge of the nose. Dad's speed and the sting of the slaps hurt, but if I covered-up I knew his open hand would close.

"Dad, I was just going to the park. Right there." I pointed as we drove by the Field House.

Blood inside my mouth made everything warm. I saw Tommy standing there with ten or so of his friends. He was shadowboxing, and I wished I could have gone just one round with him. I would have killed him right now. Knocked his faking head off. I was tough back then. But it had nothing to do with me. Dad taught me how to be tough. You see, if you could take Dad's punches, you could take anybody's.

Back at the house, things really went south. Dad told Mom to get out of the house, told her to take the car and not come back for an hour. You know, when Dad wore his berserk eyes, you just did what he said. No sense in asking why, cause the wrecking ball would take you down too. Back then, it was like being in a war-zone. Survival was your only obligation. Survival was the only constant, it propelled you. It gave you something to do. I don't ever fault Mom for leaving that day, she was a victim and there ain't nothin' fake about being a victim.

Dad pulled the kitchen chair into the middle of the floor and ordered me to sit. I did. And even when he left for what seemed fifteen minutes, I never thought about bolting. But I should have.

Finally, Dad came back up the stairs. In one hand, he had gray duct tape and his face wore a "I got you now" grin. And you know I was much more scared of Dad than I was of two Tommy Parks.

"Lesson time. Put your hands down on the arm rest," he ordered.

Dad proceeded to tape my wrist tight as possible to each of the armrests. Then my ankles. Then my mouth and nose. I couldn't breathe. He loved it. I'll never forget the sick, insane look in his eyes. Demonic almost, his eyes glowed red in the very center.

"Now, let me show you what happens when the "bogeyman" picks you up thumbing, Jakie boy!"

I knew the crap was on the wall when Dad opened the second drawer below the sink. I knew my youth was over when he slowly pulled out Mom's new, double-blade, electric carving knife. I watched him, petrified, setting it up— lining up the two jagged-edges, pushing the red button, and inserting the blades. My thoughts boiled in scalding-hot anxiety when I saw him plug the cord in over the toaster. But I never flinched until I heard the sound of the blades humming in perfect formation. I squeezed my eyes real tight, but the humming only penetrated deeper. The darker it got on the back of my eyelids, the faster the blades seemed to run. I never felt the blades hitting the finish line. It was the humming that I'll always remember. It dulled as the blades cut my left arm between my shoulder and elbow.

I opened my eyes and saw Jesus watching from his cross on the kitchen wall. Blood splashed the floor and walls like tiny, tiny rain drops in a windstorm. But no faking, I can just never recall the physical pain. It was the mental thing that's forever real for me. Dad standing there with his lips moving to a silent Hail Mary verse. He was saying the rosary, his eyes, holding that knife, staring into the back of my brain. The first cut was all, and it was more like a pinch than a hurt. The flesh jumped open and created a gaping slit a good inch deep. I could see a white jell, and purple paste. There was no blood. I couldn't scream for help. I just prayed for this lesson to end.

"Okay, Jake, now it's time for the Jugular Vein."

And that's when I started to cry. Dad saw my tears and turned the volume up on the Hail Marys. The Rosary turned into a chant. The louder I sobbed, the louder I heard— "Thy will be done." When Dad put down the knife I thought Christ had saved me. But then Dad took the duct tape and completely covered my eyes. Nothing but gray.

I remember hearing the knife click on. But I didn't panic. I actually felt peaceful all over; kinda like the way I always did after a good cry. The sound got louder. I sensed the dead-space between the knife and my neck getting smaller. I started laughing hysterical, right through the tape forcing my mouth closed. A warm tingle raced down my legs as piss pooled in my sneakers. The cold steel touched my neck right below my Adam's Apple.

It was a trick. Dad had touched my throat with the dull side of the blade.

It took thirty-two stitches to close my arm. Dad made up a story, and I backed him. Two weeks later, I put Tommy Sparks in the hospital over night— broke his jaw and nose.

I still got the scar. And sometimes in the middle of the night it burns like the wound is open again. It reminds me of stitches on my old football. In the cold air it turns pinkish-purple and in Maine's ocean water the jagged line becomes midnight-blue.

Today, I can't escape one night without hearing the hum of the knife closing around me. Do you really think Dad thought cutting me would save me someday from bad things?

I mean—Dad was the "bogeyman."

Chath Piersath

THE WAY I WANT TO REMEMBER MY CAMBODIA

I want to remember how I was free to run in the field
eyeing the sky—my handmade kite flying high,
loving the wind, loving the clear white cloud.

I want to remember how I was free to run in the sun,
free to own and roam the fields, free to walk and sing
to myself or to God of the hills full of trees, to the green
rice paddies, to the pink lotus in my pond, and to the black
muddy swamp, to the white crystal tune of an overflowing
river, to the rainbow of my felicity and the wild dogs' red
mating call.

I want to feel the flirtatious air caressing my naked body
in childhood innocence wrapped in the arms of my brothers,
free of hate, free of war.

I want to remember the shrilling cry of crickets hidden
under broken planks, the way I went earring for them
in the mist of dawn to capture them in my jar. My chase
after dragonflies, my sling pebbles passing birds, how I
spent day after day fishing, netting grasshoppers in the sun,
and in its burning heat, how I went searching for beetles in
cow manure while herding cattle and water buffalo
away from home.

I recall my mother's cooking fire, her salted fish grilled
on burning charcoal, the smell of her boiling stew, her
sharp knife drumming the cutting board. In her outdoor
kitchen, the smoke of her art hissed out of her wok, moving
into the air like a cobra shedding its skin on our fence.

I want to feel my dark Cambodian skin crack from playing
with earth, my boyish brown eyes to stare again at the green
bamboo, leaning to soak in the fragrance of the yellow, flowered
hills. I want the serenity of the blue ponds and the white river of
childhood and to feel the winds wiping away the dewdrops,
still clinging to my naked body.

I want my peasant home, to still be in that village among
the surviving people on that laboring earth where I was born
into my Cambodia.

My Cambodia, tell me again the stories of how the old
ghosts take possession of human souls, how monsters
shape the art of death. I want to hear how the Goddesses
turn what is ugly into what is beautiful.
Make me part of that secret. Let me dance in your sun.

Brian T. O'Brien

SHELL SHOCK

(William O'Brien served with The Royal Munster Fusiliers from 1902-1919.)

I found an oyster shell along the coast,
more pock-marked, scarred, and pitted than most
other oyster wracks tossed by the surf
upon this slender beach I claim as my turf.
It's been my comfort to gather the shells
of whelks, whose spirals, like the Book of Kells'
illuminate letters, demonstrated
a provident deity created
nature's bounty. But this thing -- broken,
bruised, misshapen -- the very token
of disposal, clean-scoured by predators
until, like the homes cleared by creditors
during the famine, nothing remained as proof
that sentient things had lived beneath the roof.

My father too was partly thrust outside
his home. "Partly" means he chose the tide
that carried him beyond the dark and damp
of Limerick, which he traded for a camp
experience with like-minded boys
not suited for guns so much as toys.
He saw the greater world, from Gibraltar
to the Khyber Pass, and didn't falter

when his king (but not his country) ordered
him to neutral Belgium (non-bordered
if, like von Schlieffen, your target is France.)
"It won't last long. You'll be home to dance
by Christmas," was the promise. But winter
saw trenches from the Channel to the hinter-
lands of Spain. At Ypres (pronounced "Wipers"),
he saw comrades shell-shocked into diapers.

'Twas damp trenches caused his grotesque toenails,
oyster shell projections, more fit for snails'
company than "human society,"
a phrase not much linked with sobriety
after he'd survived Wipers and Gallipoli.
War medals I've framed don't capture him fully.
But this shell, pocked, scarred, and broken
speaks truer of him than any bronze token.

Brian T. O'Brien

CALLING THE SWAN

So, when the last and dreadful hour
This crumbling pageant shall devour,
The Trumpet shall be heard on high,
The dead shall live, the living die,
And Music shall untune the sky.
  John Dryden, "A Song for St. Cecilia's Day"

At my last breath, I pray
some loving friend will play
or sing such music as may
comfort my contentious soul
and guide it to eternity.

Could I choose, I'd hear again
music that I can't repeat,
played for me one winter day
in a snowscape by a bay—
fresh-laid white, which that dawn lay
glimmering. From a cut
in the mantled salt marsh—
thawed, woven, and refrozen—
of such varied shapes and textures
that it seemed itself alive,
frigid earth's white womb had birthed
a miraculous white bird
that overflew my head
and overwhelmed my wonder.

It was a passing over
(such a close encounter—
a matter of a foot or less)
to accelerate the pulse
and send me sprawling.

That should have been enough
to make me mindful of
the gulf which, after Eden,
keeps our fellowship with nature
arm's length despite our longing;
but even more, its music,
momentous yet eternal,
comprising and surpassing
fear, longing, and chill March winds.
The swan (was it cob or pen?),
filtering the frosty air
through its outstretched pinions,
fashioned music that both gods—
of harp and pipe—might envy,
an instrument at once
blown and plucked and struck
that played its way to eternity
and quite untuned the winter sky.

Thus I try, like a throat singer
from the plateaus of Tibet,
to inflate my fearful spirit
and overtone the ocean's roar.
So were two mutes unmuted.

Mehmed Ali

HAIKU OUT OF MY WINDOW

light sleet falls
on the Laotian
woman's face
who remembers home

canals run
like moats around the
castles
of cotton kings

empty mills
littered like fallen bird's nests
whose owners flew south

Lois Frankenberger

LOST & FOUND IN CAMBRIDGE

They unpacked a couple of suitcases
in a room with a brass bed, with a bathroom
at the end of the hall three flights up
on 11 Trowbridge Street. A few blocks down
they opened a coffee house on Plimpton Street.
Called it Café Mozart. Each day they'd walk up
the steps dividing them from the Gold Coast Valeteria,
headed for the kitchen, where she diced, chopped,
boiled and brewed, while he filled the front room's need
for an excuse to linger, read,
speak about issues religious, political
at marble-topped tables
over schlage-topped coffee,
sandwiches and lapsang souchong tea,
their voices walled in by brass samovars
filtered through Mozart and scattered
until one night she sat with a stranger
and he talked to her as if she mattered.

Ben Hellman

THE BLACK MAMBA

A Comedy about Love and Survival

(*Lights come up, but remain dim on the living room of Fred and Eileen Wannamaker. Fred is sitting in his recliner reading the paper. A large serving bowl is overturned and lying in the center of the floor. The lights rise for the opening of the scene.*)

Announcer.
> The Black Mamba. It is considered by many to be the deadliest snake in the world. It has earned this reputation from its extraordinary speed and an extremely potent poison that disables its victim's nervous system. But while the Mamba's lightning speed and potent poison are unmatched in the animal kingdom, it is the snake's short temper and quickness to strike, which have earned it the fear and respect of snake experts. Recorded attacks show that a cornered Black Mamba will attack multiple targets and bite repeatedly before retreating. No other snake can match the aggressive nature of the Black Mamba.

Eileen. (*Enters from kitchen*) Fred, where is my serving bowl?!?

Fred. (*Stopping her*) Eileen, be very still-

Eileen. No, Fred, no! Not tonight-

Fred.   I'm very serious Eileen.

Eileen. No, Fred, that is exactly the problem, you are never serious. Now I need my serving bowl.

Fred.   Eileen, you have no idea how much danger we're in. Stay close to me.

Eileen. Fred, what are you doing? You have to get ready. I need to take my serving bowl.

Fred.   Eileen, I've trapped a very large, very mean snake under that bowl.   I think it's stunned, but any sudden movements or vibrations and it will easily topple the bowl.

Eileen. Fred, I've had enough of this. We need to get ready.

Fred.   (*Quickly*) Why?

Eileen. You know why.

Fred.   No, I don't.

Eileen. Yes, you do.

Fred.   No, I don't.

Eileen. Yes, you do.

Fred.   No, I don't. (*he pinches her before she can finish*)

Eileen. Yes, yo—(*she shrieks*)

Fred.   Why do they have to come over tonight?

Eileen. Fred, it's their anniversary! You've known about this. I told you about this. What is your problem?

Fred.   I thought we could have a nice quiet evening together tonight.

Eileen. We will have a nice quiet evening, just the four of us. Now I need my bowl.

Fred. Eileen, I'm warning you. Do not touch that bowl.

Eileen. I'm taking the bowl, Fred.

Fred. Eileen, I will tackle you if you get one step closer. Do you want to break the bowl?

Eileen. Fred, that bowl was a wedding present from my parents. If you break that bowl, it's all over.

Fred. I don't want you to break the bowl, but I think that we should have a talk about us.

Eileen. Now is not the time, Fred.

Fred. When is the time, Eileen? I try to speak to you in the morning and you're going to be late for work. I try to speak to you at night and you're too tired. So what I'm asking you is when can we speak about this?

Eileen. Fred, it is my parent's fiftieth wedding anniversary. I am their only child. I promised them a nice dinner with us tonight. The roast is in the oven. The vegetables are on the stove and I need that bowl. You can see that I don't have the time.

Fred. When are you going to have the time for us, Eileen?!? When are you going to have the time for *us*!?

Eileen. Stop yelling at me!

Fred. Eileen, I am trying to be grown up about his, but you are making it very hard.

Eileen. I am taking my bowl, Fred, I am finishing dinner.

Fred. You don't love me.

Eileen. What?!

Fred.   You don't love me.

Eileen. How can you say that, you're my husband!?

Fred.   And yet, you don't love me.

Eileen. How can you say that to me Fred, how can you say it!?

Fred.   If you ever made the slightest attempt at showing me you loved me, things wouldn't have gotten this far.

Eileen. I do things for you all the time.

Fred.   Do you ever say 'I love you, Fred'?

Eileen. Yes.

Fred.   When was the last time you said it?

Eileen. All the time.

Fred.   No you don't. You take it for granted that I know these things, but you never say the words.

Eileen. I don't believe you're doing this to me now.

Fred.   Tell me you love me.

Eileen. There's no time!

Fred.   Tell me you love me. (*He puts his hands on her arms and holds her in a smothering embrace.*)

Eileen. Fred—

Fred. I'm not going to let you go, Eileen!

(*There is a brief struggle. She elbows and punches at his body, and he simply allows it while holding on.*)

Eileen. Let go, let go, let go! What do you want from me!?

Fred.   Do you love me!?

Eileen. (*She breaks free with a violent shove*) Yes! Yes, I love you. You're my husband, you're my mate. Of course, I love you. I love you. (*Tears stream down her face, Fred moves in tenderly and holds her as she breaks down.*) Don't leave me.

Fred. I'm not going to leave you. I love you. I just want to know you love me too.

Eileen. Of course I love you. You're my husband. I love you. (*More embracing, they kiss*) I'm going to have to change now and fix my face, they'll be here any minute. Can I have the bowl now?

Fred. Yes, of course. (*Fred lifts the serving bowl and an angry Black Mamba leaps out, strikes both of them and scurries under the recliner. It all happens very quickly and as Fred and Eileen collapse to the floor they pull close to each other and hold each other. The lights start to dim.*)

Announcer.

Fred and Eileen Wannamaker. A married couple with ordinary fears and human frailties. When their love for each other was tested and they were faced with the prospect of losing each other's companionship they show their instincts for protection and survival. But even so they are no match for the Black Mamba.

The End

Caroline K Kemp

STERILE

With its legs crushed and bloody,
the rabbit lay still in the nighttime wake

of the speeding car, waves of dust settling
on the sidewalk, the cat's eyes gleaming

stealthily as it strode forward from the bushes.
At the little Chinese restaurant covered with

Red lanterns, I pull open my fortune cookie—
"the stars are shining in the sky;

all is well"—and put half of the brown shell
onto my tongue while twirling the little brown paper.

Hello, I whisper to myself in China
that would be *ni hao*; but amid

the throngs of brightly colored polyester and
cheap souvenirs in Beijing, I cannot see the stars.

Hidden behind purple handmade veils,
Afghan women are forbidden to vote,

to drive, to wear makeup, even to
try to touch the stars with a kite

quivering above the barren fields.
I know the stars are hidden there,

but how do I know this
if the stars cannot be touched? God too,

where is he / she when looking out from
my television are the haunted eyes

of a four-year old in Somalia, her arms
and legs tucked into her hollow rib cage

like a baby sparrow fallen from its nest
"Blood is a medicine that cannot be

manufactured," and yet still no one gives;
I, holding my mother's hand in the

sterile doctor's office, have been shot with
anesthesia against my will, numbed to

the poverty in India, where the homeless
walk around holding long-dead babies

and perform amputations to beg more money.
I have traveled to see the Great Wall and bought

jade Buddhas in the marketplace, so I know that
ni hao ma means how are you, but

without the stars I don't know who I am,
so I turn away and do nothing, crying

while it lies on the dripping grass and
closing my porch door on the rabbit and its cat.

Andre Dubus III

SHOE CITY

A novel

PART ONE

Even from the flat roof of Shotz's Brewery you could smell the river: the sewer pipes and spilled oil and gas, the hot mud of the banks drying in the sun where there were clothes all twisted up, dirty rocks sticking up out of the silt, shoes or boots, shopping carts lying on their sides, whole car engines rusted browner than the river which always had a current in it; even on hot summer afternoons you could see the water swirling by fast. Nobody took a boat out on it or tried to fish. On both sides was a high concrete wall, and farther down was the steel bridge named after the first kid from town to get killed in that war everybody said was almost over. His name was something LaPierre, and it was called The LaPierre Bridge.

Cleary was sitting against one of the chimney stacks drinking from a Schlitz Tall Boy, looking hard at his dirty magazine. Sean's beer tasted good, not too warm out of the basement where they got it right after they dropped through the window a grown man could never get through. It had pigeon shit and wire over it, but it swung open every time, and the brewery only seemed to have people working in it two or three days a week. Sometimes Sean and Cleary would stay there in the basement and hear them loading trucks up above while they sat on a damp pallet in the dark, drinking a six-pack. When the building was empty, they came to the roof.

Sean walked over and looked down at Cleary's magazine. The man was kneeling behind the woman and Sean thought how the pictures never looked like it felt, that the whole world was warm and sweet and God wanted you to like life. Love it even. He wanted to try Rae's again. Soon it'd be Saturday night. You could see it in the sun on the sides of the mills, the way the bricks looked a golden red. Rae's old lady waitressed all day and night downtown, then she'd go drinking after. They could have her whole bed to themselves.

He finished his beer and got another. It always tasted the best when the day was hot and your stomach was empty and you'd been thirsty a long time. There were some words under the pictures in Cleary's magazine, and he was running his finger under each one, moving his lips. At his house was only one book. It was called **The Illustrated Bible**. His mother kept it on the coffee table where she put her vodka and OJ and his old man rested his stocking-covered feet, his work boots on a piece of cardboard on the floor back in the kitchen. They watched a lot of TV. The first time Cleary was in Sean's house, he said he'd never seen that many books in his life. He asked whose they were, and Sean told him his old man left them behind and Cleary didn't say anything else, just stood there looking at them all. Last winter Sean read one, a whole book by a Russian about peasants and all they used to do over there. He liked being them. It was good not being him for a while.

Cleary burped. "What's this word, Dole?" Sean leaned closer. "Velvety."

"What's that?"

Sean read the whole sentence about the man pushing himself into the woman's velvety love canal. "You know, that soft fuzzy shit women like. Clothes."

"She's got <u>clothes</u> in her?" Cleary was squinting up at him in one of his old man's white t-shirts and his fake jeans and cheap sneakers. Sean could see he wasn't joking. Sometimes he wanted to walk away from him and never look back.

"They're saying it's as soft as those clothes." He almost said *moron* or *dumb shit*, but everybody called him that already. Sean sat down on the other side of the chimney and took a long hit off his beer. His buzz was back better than before when Rae and Trina weren't home, and he and Cleary drank what they'd brought them. Just past the projects' rusted dumpster that smelled like hot steel and old welfare cheese, Cleary'd opened the bottle of Southern Comfort, and they passed it back and forth on their way through the gravel lot and past the high weeds to the buckled sidewalk of Seventh Avenue. There were houses with crooked porches. Everybody was sick of the war, but still, stuck to a lot of windows were faded decals of the American flag. Some of the yards had grass, some didn't. Around them were chain link fences, a few guard dog signs nobody paid attention to. There weren't any trees on the street, and Sean had thought of Trina's sister Rae, fourteen like him, with her curly black hair and small breasts and that tiny mole just above her pubic hair, a little bump you had to get by on the way down.

The last of the sun felt good on his face and even the river smelled okay. He closed his eyes, the bricks nice and warm on his back, but there was that sadness again. It was coming up on him more and more. Even when he was with Cleary, he felt far away from him and everybody. Sometimes he'd try to remember when he didn't feel this way. Maybe when he was six or seven and Pop still lived with them, the four of them sitting around the kitchen table eating fried chicken, LuAnn with a barrette in her hair, smiling or laughing at everything their old man ever said. Now all she wore was hip huggers her stomach was just a little too big for, black or blue t-shirts, a pack of Kools in the pocket. Both wrists were covered with cheap silver bracelets she got at the beach or lifted downtown, and she wore blue eye shadow that made her look like a slut, always squinting at him through the smoke of her cigarette like he was the loser all her fuck head friends said he was.

Down on Water Street somebody was revving an engine. The doors to the bars were open. A lady laughed. Some men were talking low. A jukebox was playing *Bad Bad Leroy Brown, the baddest man in the whole damn town.* Soon it'd be fall again, then winter, the worst season because nobody had anywhere to go, so a lot of them hung out in the house with his sister. He'd come home in the afternoon and smell the dope before he even opened the door. The record player their mother's last boyfriend bought her would be playing too loud, The Stones or Alice Cooper. The front room would be full of smoke, and Nick Gifano'd be lying on the wicker couch with his wet boots on, taking the whole thing up himself Butts Rayco would be swigging from a bottle, his stringy hair stuck behind his ears, looking out at everybody with small black eyes. LuAnn usually sat on the floor next to Gifano's face, smoking. There'd be chicks from the projects across the street sitting back against the walls, their leather jackets still on, the hems of their hip huggers wet from the sidewalk slush. Gifano would say, "Fag boy's home", and a few might look up; sucking deep on their cigarette or joint. Sean'd go into the kitchen, three or four of them sitting at the table playing 45, smelling like wet leather and spilled beer, bubble gum and smoke. He'd go right past them up to his room, shut the door, turn his clock radio up loud. He might try to do some homework or just lie there on his bed thinking about throwing them all out, being tough enough to do it himself, just pick up each and every one of them and toss them out the door onto Seventh Avenue.

Cleary opened another beer. "Last one, Dole. Wanna get some more?"

Sean thought about walking home loaded, how much farther a walk it was then. Plus he was hungry. "Got any cash?"

"Nope. You?"

"Why would I ask you if I did?" "I don't know."

Sean finished off his beer and threw the can against the short wall that looked out over the rest of town, the railroad bridge cutting over the square that was nothing but brick mill buildings eight or nine stories high. Some of the top floor windows were covered with plywood. On the bottom were all the barrooms, the shops nobody went into. They had gray metal fronts or fake brick, and their picture windows were full of dusty displays with a broken light or two. The owners were old men and women who'd been here when the river wasn't so polluted and families strolled along the sidewalk and stepped into the clean stores for shiny goods. There weren't any welfare projects or people who only spoke Spanish or long-haired punks like Sean; that's how Cleary's old man always talked about the town before. He wore white t-shirts that showed off his Navy tattoos, blue work pants even when he wasn't at his job down in Boston working for the Transit Authority, whatever that was. Cleary said his old man would whack his mother or him and his younger brother when he got mad but only when he'd really had it. Most of the time he sat in front of the TV. On top of it was the framed picture of Cleary's older brother dressed in his Marines uniform with the American flag behind him.

Cleary walked over to the river side of the roof and pissed off it. Sean had to go too. Shotz's moved a little when he got up, and he had to hop once to stay in his boots. Two tall ones and he was half –drunk, and he always felt small and weak when it happened that fast, and it always did. He stood next to Cleary and pissed down to the alley where there were stacks of crates covered with pigeon shit, and he knew they'd just pissed right by the window and were going to have to put their bare hands on it when they pulled themselves up. He laughed and Cleary did too, though he didn't know why.

On the other side of the water was a line of pigeons standing on the river wall. Past them were weeds and pricker bushes covering the slope all the way up to the backs of the fast food restaurants up there. Three of them side by side. Sometimes you could find a bag of burgers they had to throw in the dumpster because they'd been under the warmer too long, but to get there they'd have to walk through town and across the LaPierre Bridge. They could take the railroad trestle, running from tie to tie, but you never knew when the train was coming, and when it did there was no place to go. Cleary's house across from Seventh was almost just as far. Inside his house his mother stayed home all day and had supper ready at six o' clock every night, and even though she was drinking most of the time and her words came out too slow, it was nice sitting at a table with a whole family like that.

Sean shook himself off and zipped up. He was weaving, which wasn't good on a roof. One of the pigeons took off then they all did, flying in different directions.

His mother's Toyota was parked on the sidewalk in front of the house. The tires had no hubcaps and on the back bumper was a sticker that said *Impeach the Mad Bomber*. The front windows were down, and on the passenger's seat was a bunch of paperwork under some empty coffee cups and French fry cartons. Her ashtray was full of butts. The sun was almost gone, her boyfriend's pickup wasn't around, and across the street at the projects somebody was laughing and couldn't stop.

Inside, his mother was sitting in front of the TV watching news about the hearings. She was smoking a cigarette and holding a milk glass full of Gallo wine. She had the fan pointed at her, her feet up on the picnic table bench they used as a coffee table. Her skirt was unbuttoned, and she'd pulled her blouse out, and Sean could see her nylons curled up in a ball by her shoes. The room was dim, and he didn't smell anything cooking. "Hey."

"Hey baby, I didn't hear you come in."

"Yeah." He stood there and watched what she was watching, a bunch of men in suits sitting in front of a microphone talking about the President and all the liars who worked for him. Pop had hated him so much, instead of saying he had to take a shit, he'd say he had to go take a Nixon. Sean's stomach felt hot and sour, and even though he and Cleary had pissed on the walk home, once behind Dunkin Donuts that smelled like sweet dough and a holiday, he had to go again.

"What's for supper?"

"I don't know, what're you cooking?" His mother smiled and took a long drag off her cigarette. He walked through the kitchen that had four days of dishes in the sink, climbed the stairs to the bathroom then lay down on his bed. His feet were hot. He pulled off his boots. There were always dishes in the sink, old fast food bags on the counter, grit all over the floor. For a while after Pop left they had chores to do, but when LuAnn wouldn't do hers, he wouldn't do his, and when he didn't do his, she never did hers, and their mother was always too tired to make them. After a while they all just got used to it, the dirt and the dust and the grease, the smell of cigarette and pot smoke in everything, moldy towels in the bathroom. Sometimes he felt bad about his mother working all the time, and he'd spend the afternoon cleaning, dusting everything with a rag, sweeping, mopping, straightening up. But then LuAnn would walk in with five or six fuckers behind her, and he'd come to his room and shut the door. He got tired of lying there though, his black light posters of Bob Dylan and Janis Joplin looking back at him. Next to her was one of a black baby in diapers. *Black is Beautiful.* His mother gave it to him a year after that black man King got shot in the head on the motel balcony.

In the corner of Sean's room was the old Daisy BB gun his old man'd given to him before Shoe City when they lived in pine trees on a hill by a pond, and he showed him how to press the stock to his cheek, how to squint his eye and line up the sights, how to hold his breath and squeeze the trigger. Sean could smell his father's aftershave, the coffee on his breath. He liked when he put his arms around him to show him the right way to aim. He shot everything with that gun: cans, bottles that cracked and shattered, tree trunks, leaves—he'd put four or five holes in each. He started shooting birds off of branches and felt trembly when he killed them, then mean and sad and a little sick to his stomach. He'd recock his rifle and walk over to the bird lying there on the ground, a wing twitching. Then he'd press the barrel to its head and shoot, watch the tiny beak jerk. He felt better and worse and like he'd seen this a thousand times already. When he was four, building a house of blocks, his mother walked in crying, wiping her eye makeup away, saying somebody shot the President. Then he was eight, and it was the black doctor. A few months later the dead President's little brother trying to be President too. It took him a while to die, and Pop kept the TV Off the whole time. They showed pictures of the man's brain, where the bullet was. Sean thought of that every time he killed a bird, the President's little brother's brain and the tiny bullet that killed it.

There were all those soldiers on the news every night right up till just a couple of years ago, dead men getting dragged through tall grass all beaten down from the helicopter blades, some of the bodies in long zipped up bags. Pop would sit there crying. "They're just boys," he'd say. "They're just boys."

Brody Pagel

THEY SAY YOU ARE SHATTERED

they say you are shattered
i prefer arranged
glimmering, ready for singing back
to the bottom of boots, sandals, tennis shoes
(hungry for bare feet)
a testament to last night
maybe you fell, maybe you were thrown
i can't help thinking you jumped
now rid of that restricting label
you lay sprawled out on cool concrete
for a clear view of the stars
i know this because you shine
excited and hopeful
emptied, but no longer hollow
for now you have eternity directly above you
you have the poetry of passers by
a symphony of sirens and car horns
(composed by no one and everyone)
if only hearts broke so beautifully

hold onto the rim when the waters begin to spill
until the world rounds the next turn.

~ Kathleen Hunkele Schardin

John Greenleaf Whittier

SWEET FERN

The subtle power in perfume found
Nor priest nor sibyl vainly learned;
On Grecian shrine or Aztec mound
No censer idly burned.

That power the old-time worships knew,
The Corybantes' frenzied dance,
The Pythian priestess swooning through
The wonderland of trance.

And Nature holds, in wood and field,
Her thousand sunlit censers still;
To spells of flower and shrub we yield
Against or with our will.

I climbed a hill path strange and new
With slow feet, pausing at each turn;
A sudden waft of west wind blew
The breath of the sweet fern.

That fragrance from my vision swept
The alien landscape; in its stead,
Up fairer hills of youth I stepped,
As light of heart as tread.

I saw my boyhood's lakelet shine
Once more through rifts of woodland shade;
I knew my river's winding line
By morning mist betrayed.

With me June's freshness, lapsing brook,
Murmurs of leaf and bee, the call
Of birds, and one in voice and look
In keeping with them all.

A fern beside the way we went
She plucked, and, smiling, held it up,
While from her hand the wild, sweet scent
I drank as from a cup.

O potent witchery of smell!
The dust-dry leaves to life return,
And she who plucked them owns the spell
And lifts her ghostly fern.

Or sense or spirit? Who shall say
What touch the chord of memory thrills?
It passed, and left the August day
Ablaze on lonely hills.

Annie Deppe

BLACK DOG BLUES

After making love, we hurry
     down the path toward the funeral
          and out comes the black dog, Sophie.

A sorry beast—someone must have
     beat her before she went to live
          with the German woman.

After her walking companion died,
     our neighbors took in Sophie. They dressed
          in the dead woman's clothes

for almost a week before the dog
     stopped shaking. Even so,
          with a cockeyed sort of wisdom

Sophie barks as we pass by.
     Today, the boat's brought
          the blind goatherd's mother for burial:

that makes three deaths
     this winter for the island.
          Even though it's not

the German woman today,
     up on the hillside Sophie howls.
          At the grave, the blindman's dog

wears a kind of a dog smile
     as it nudges its master
          back from the edge.

Len Krisak

THE DEER AT THE END OF THE ROAD

March morning dark, and only now he sees

The lights that shape some kind of Christmas fawn

Fixed on the graveled cul-de-sac's last lawn.

The Yule's receding tide has set this here

To outline emptiness, then let it freeze,

He thinks, the inner spaces of the deer

As solid in their blinking topiary

As any bronze not half so stilly posed.

How could mere glowing lines appear unwary,

The hind's heart so apparent thus enclosed?

A certain trick of light, he must surmise,

To trace such poise upon the morning's brink

And so transfix this early walker's eyes,

Which lift as Lucifer begins to wink.

Frances McCormick

WALKING ON STILTS

through hovering summer hours, under sun-dappled green
& heat-heavy
maples, on pebble-scattered paths, &, daringly, up
concrete steps

our brown freckled hands,
grasping
the long poles, strong but thin enough for a child's
hand to hold

our scuffy play shoes, laces half-undone,
held carefully on
the wedges of wood, wide as a small foot,
uncomfortable under the arch

we stilt-walked, stiff-legged, scabbed knees rigid,
wary of the sudden shift of surface, the precarious
balance threatened
my brother the bold leader, my sister equal to the
challenge, & me

we built our stilts, scrap wood & hammer & nails, tho?
screws were better

learning how to teeter, tackle fear & relish the rarer
air up there
launching off from stone walls, the momentum a
propellant
into the dizzying rush of triumph

more than half a century later we stilt-walk still,
bravely, as if over thin ice
or dangerous chasms, the heights greater, the stride
wider, dusk descending
our hours hovering, waning, slipping away

our elusive dreams, our pressing duties & endless
ambitions the constant fuel
that keeps us eternally, joyously, fearfully,
innocently, carefully, courageously
walking on stilts

Gaby Uberto Beltre

MORE LIKE AN ANGEL

I just got off a ride. I saw tons of people walking in different directions, some eating candy apples and others conversing.

"What ride should we get on?" My boy shrugged. I looked at the Blizzard. And then I looked at the Bumper Cars. And then I looked t the Cobra. Then right there I saw a girl.

"Who's that? I asked, my heart beating quickly as if I had seen a ghost. But it wasn't. It was more like an angel.

"I have to see who's that." I said

"Who?" my boy, Charlie, asked.

"Her, right there."

Charlie noticed who I was talking about. "Oh, she does look good," he said.

She disappeared in the crowd right before I could go up to her and talk to her.

"Damn, where did she go?" I asked

"I don't know. But don't worry though, you'll find her later." Then Charlie and I started walking.

Later, I saw her again. This time I could not let her get away.

"Yo, Charlie. I'll be back." I started walking slowly towards her. Right then three or four girls went up to her and said, "Let's get on the Sea Dragon." I kept on walking. I walked right past her making it seem like I was walking somewhere else.

But as I walked past her, I saw her staring at me from the corner of my eye.

"Damn, I couldn't talk to her," I said to Charlie.

"Why not?" Charlie asked.

"Nah, because she's with them girls."

"So who cares?" Charlie said.

"Nah, I just want to talk to her by herself. But don't worry. I'll get the chance later."

Later that day, I saw her. This time she was by herself. She was standing next to the water fountain. This was my chance to finally talk to her. So I started to approach her. As I approached her, I stated in to her eyes.

"Wasup. What's your name?"

"Diana."

"Diana, oh, wasup. I'm Gaby. So wasup, you here by yourself?"

"Nah, I'm here with my girls. They're over there by the hotdog stand."

"Oh, so wasup, can I get your number?"

"Sure" She gave me her number.

"No doubt. I'll holla at you later."

I gave a look, then I bounced.

Michele Leavitt

CHARM SCHOOL

Of course, it was unbearable
To me, as I was awkwardly
Between the flat, intractable
Self that's called a child, and the curvy
Mystery of a woman's need
To please. My mother paid for me
To go. We were taught about nice looks
And modest posture, how to feed
Our surfaces with creams, how books
Could give us wrinkles, how to cope
With rudeness and direct attack
submissively. And now, friends hope
My mother got her money back.

Michele Leavitt

ME AND MY BITCH

You've seen those dogs resembling
their masters; that's not us. Her sordid past
is commonplace: while circling
a cozy den she'd made beneath a cast-
off car, she landed at the pound.
That's where we met and where she came to love
me desperately. The dogs I've wound
up with have all been strays with histories,
and this one knows the value of
a snarl, bared teeth. She has her policies:
since loving just invites great loss,
expect the very worst and guard what's dear;
it's always best to act the boss
when scavenging some fearsomeness from fear.

Kathleen Hunkele Schardin

NEPTUNE

Thrown from stone-polished rivers and churning storms,
at every side a blow,
hairy ropes of gray and white unravel
to drag the slate water underground,
breathe death-filled air where
nibbling creatures arise from crackling strands of sea ribbon
and foam,
and rush to meet us in the cascade of life falling together.

Nuggets now, smooth like pearls, drop from heaven,
given as if the One sent mantras through this god
to enlarge and wizen the globe -

"The stones the prophets ate are bread for you too,
the dust of planets sits full
weaving stories of watery mountains and beaten
shores that sift the grain,
tucking gems among the shells."

Open-mouthed inside the earth,
turned under the crescent edge,
eyes to the sky while polishing oceans arch our backs,
hold onto the rim when the waters begin to spill
until the world rounds the next turn.

Dave Gardner

THE HANGAR

The vast roads of Western Mass were a welcomed change from the grids back home that lay tribute to some thin necked engineer who had long since moved away. It was very dark and the rain had just stopped coming down on the road. Streetlight had led to humming streetlight for a long, long time. On and on we drove, my brother and myself, listening to the water under the spinning tires, watching as each lonesome hanging light came and receded into night behind us. We were going to meet his girlfriend Una to have some drinks and go find a party back on campus.

"You'll like this place" he said, and he went on driving. We didn't see each other much anymore, because he was away at school, but he never seemed to change too much. His face had a strong shape like mine, but he had a short beard that I never could grow. His eyes were large and dark.

We reached the town limits of Amherst, and kept driving. There was nothing but road and lights and woods on either side. The leaves were turning early this season, and the wind pushed them all around.

Not much farther up the road, a place came into view. Neon signs from the windows made neon figures in the puddles in the lot out front. I watched them dance and twist around, until they disappeared when we got too close. A brown sign swung from a chain above the front door. It read "The Hangar". The building was cozy, built in the style of a ski-lodge, with a big triangular roof that hung over the rough wood sides. A warm light pulsed inside.

Una waited in the parking lot in her black Acura. She came out to meet us, and we stood there in the lot, wet and chilly enough to dress as if it were winter. She was covered from head to toe in thick layered clothes.

"Hey sweetie." She pecked my brother and gave me a hug. She was a bubbly type of girl, with a full chest and an exaggerated smile. She wore a puffy white jacket and jeans and red mittens, which matched her long straight red hair. I had a picture of her in my head, leaning slightly to the side, holding on to my brother's arm. They'd been a couple for two years, and I'd had my share of tagging along in their nights out. There was no awkwardness.

We stood for a minute on the curb, observing the place where the two had kicked off so many hazy nights. They both seemed to expect a response from me, but I was watching the neon creatures in their tiny puddles.

"I like what they've done with the place" I finally remarked. I offered a smirk to their satisfaction and we walked inside.

"Its just a cool place to sit and fill up and not think about anything," Adam said as we pulled back our chairs and sat down at a table in the back. The chairs were a light colored wood with black leather pillows, really bar stools with backrests. The tables were a darker color wood, littered with scratches and marks. I could picture the place being a college bar forty years ago.

"A gin and orange juice please." Una made a small glass gesture with her fingers.

"For me too," my brother said.

I ordered a rum and coke. I wasn't legal but no one said anything or shifted eyes. It was a good honest place. The people were very real, dressed in football jerseys and caps, noisy and drunk.

"So where are we headed to anyways," I asked.

"Good question," Adam replied.

"There's a kegger over at South-West," Una suggested. "We could check that out."

"Sure." I said. The room was thick with heat and smoke and the smell of spilled beer. The neon ads in the windows were dull and the televisions flashed small fuzzy pictures in the upper corners of the bar.

"You alright?" My brother asked.

"I'm fine." I said.

"Dave you look sad."

"I'm not sad."

"Tell me?"

"I'm not sad. I promise."

"It's because you're empty kid." Adam said. "Finish that drink and then we'll order more." I did what he said. After a while the room began to leave my mind. The noise faded, and the colors blended gently. We ordered drinks again, and again, and again.

"One more year of high school kid. How's the female situation?" My brother asked.

"There is no female situation," I answered.

"You should get cute girl for yourself, Dave. You really should," Una said. She smiled her big white smile at me.

"I don't know."

"You have no idea how alike we are man. When I was in high school it was the same thing with me. You know girls get smarter as you go along, it's not worth worrying about."

"I'm not worried." I said.

"You're just wasted man, lets just finish these and we'll find somewhere better to go," He said.

Behind us the door cracked open and strolling in with a wave of cold air came a woman, aged but not old, worn thin and wrinkled with wiry black curls and loud lipstick.

I could not hear the woman's voice but saw her lips move, talking to the waitress. She walked lightly to the table behind us where she sat down. Over my brothers shoulder I could see her black hair glistening in the neon and her shape in her tight black shirt. Her black coat covered a low cut black shirt. She was thin and must have been very pretty as a girl. She sat under a hanging red light that made shadows on her face. An orange glow shifted on her table, the red light shining through her scotch as she twisted the ice cubes with long elegant fingers. She lit a cigarette. There was a coolness to her, and I was infatuated with it. Her hands demanded attention, the way she smoked and drank and patted the ash into the tray. She pouted her lips and applied some lipstick. She must have been waiting for someone.

"What are you looking at?" my brother asked. The noise in the room seemed to have gone.

"No idea."

"You look like an ass." He said.

"I wasn't staring." I replied.

The floorboards tick-tocked around in a gentle circle. The music on the jukebox began to sound like noise. I was still looking at the woman in the black shirt. She toyed with her hair, and I made up stories in my mind that could explain why she was here. She still stared at her glass and the colors on the table with her dark eyes, remembering.

The door swung open and the cold air came in again. Two little boys, both with black hair and dark eyes ran in noisily.

The two kids ran around the corner and put quarters into a video game. Soon one of the older men working the bar came out and stood behind them, obviously the father. She was probably waiting for her husband to get off work I thought. But watching the kids for a while, I realized they were not her children. She was alone, still at her table, old and bored, drinking scotch with ice and nothing else. She looked very lonely. The make up that was made to diminish the lines on her face had just the opposite effect. The flesh that curled around her mouth had been divided by a thick line of powder and years of cigarettes. I had forgotten Una and Adam. I had lost them in the noise and the heat.

"We should go," Adam finally said. "We're all drunk and we've stayed too long, we don't want to stay here too long. I paid for that, kid, you better finish it." I did as I was told and gulped the rest of my drink.

"Ok," Una said waking up. Her eyes opened and glistened clear blue. She beamed her smile at me. "It's time to get out of here."

I looked at the woman in black one last time as I stood up. I wanted her to see me watching, but she didn't. She was just like a ghost, hanging around and hanging around. It made me sad.

I tugged my coat over my shoulders and zipped it up. My feet found the way to the door behind Adam and Una. The air was freezing as we stepped outside. We waited at the door to discuss where next to. Out on the pavement over the curb the little men, pink and green and blue still shook and danced, taunting and teasing before they disappeared.

"Alright" my brother said stumbling, with Una hanging off of him. "Lets go back to campus and find a party." He was trying not to act drunk. The fresh wind blew in with the smell of moist leaves. I was happy to be rid of the smell inside.

"I don't think I'm up to it tonight man."

"What's wrong?" I buried my hands in my pockets and thought about what was wrong.

"I'm not sure." I said after a moment. He smiled serenely as if he understood.

"You're drunk kid, you just need to get some sleep." He laughed. The words went through me. I felt thin and empty, somehow robbed and brushed off; a naïve child. It lasted only a moment. He was my brother.

"Yeah." I said. "You're right." I heard my own voice become hearty again. We both had that same thick voice.

"Here's the key," he told me, opening his hand. "Go back to my dorm and get some sleep."

"Sorry." I said. "It's just not my night tonight."

"You're thinking too much kid, that's your problem."

I took the key from him. As I started to walk by the side of The Hangar I considered that maybe that *was* my problem. In through the windows I could see the guys drinking beer and the girls acting sweet. Everyone milling around, drinking and smoking in some beat up bar in Western Mass.

"No big deal," I said aloud. And on the way across the lot I lifted my head and sucked the cool air. It was a beautiful night. The wetness on the leaves shone silvery black near the streetlights. Across the road the trees blew in violent unison. I shivered at the sight of them, blown to and fro all night in the rain, firmly planted with great fists clenched underground. I looked up at them and felt the air on my face as it came. When I was ready I walked to the car, unlocked the door, and sat down inside on the leather. For a moment I felt empty again, sitting there in my brothers car in the parking lot of a bar at night. I opened the sunroof and sat for a while, not thinking, or hoping, or caring, just sitting. Finally it was time to go. I started the engine, turned towards the road, and drove home alone in the dark.

Patricia Callan

ODE TO THE VIOLIN

Listen now
to the violin,
curved mistress
of the woodshop.
How the world swoons
at her call.

Ballerina
on vibrating feet
luring her bowing,
pizzicato acolytes,
the orchestra.
She pitches ridicule at their heads.
She wounds without words,
Spiraling up up up
off the starlit fingerboard,
screaming like a Roman candle
soaring to the celestial pinwheel.

Devil instrument,
itinerant prodigy,
she is diva — brags
about her lovers,
how they caress her,
how she flees
before they can bite.

Her comforting
is prayer,
is a procession
to the pyramids.
Cremona. Amati.
Guarneri. Stradivari.
Tree. Stain. Wine.
Water. Blood
and truth.

Patricia Callan

MAMMOGRAM

In chairs against the wall we wait
Each year, the day we would forego.
I compare and count us — eight
Whose genes allow the body blow.
Wearing the clinic's pink and blue
(Beneath our robes some scarred, some not)
Breastless Amazon daughters who
Flush our quarry, hunt a spot
Unknown, unthought. This is a space
Where no one speaks of time or fright
And hope attends the patient face.
They take my portrait, stroked in light
Of tracings, shadows, lumps of fear;
To be reprieved for one more year.

Greg Waters

INFANCY ABRIDGED
for Luke

Theophilus would be amazed by you,
unready but already working
hard at life. You're writing the Acts
as you see them; a view from within,
before and beyond. You know more,
having experienced tumult, eyeing
the meadow though tethered
to the jungle, choking on your chain.
Peace comes in pieces too fragile
to remember, like drops of desert rain.
Pain, a rogue wave, surprises.
We find faith in strange states,
praying for boldness to prove our worth.
Soon the Apostles will understand
the importance of your presence here.

Greg Waters

DESCENDENT DREAMING

I dream her descended,
emerging into meadow
vested in Edelweiss—
rarely found and seldom
seen—germinated within
the rock face cracks.
Bloom short-lived,
its stem a thread, it waits
for my grandmother
there

who dreams her home,
while plucking dandelions
here

Mark Schorr

SHOCK AND RECOGNITION

1

While others dug for black gold,
my father was a telegraph boy
who rode a delivery bike
and later dug a grease pit
for a Ford dealer named Jenkins
to earn enough to pay
for his first car; we knew

this much in family lore
(unless my father made it up)
but none of it was verified
by me until two years before
my father died, once upon a time,
while paging through a year book
of the town where he had lived
when he was sixteen, I found
him in a picture that placed
him in the life of that town

& there in the front row
in a lineup of telegraph boys
was this unmistakable view
of that place, in this society
where we become our own
admirers before we finally
come to an understanding
of what we can become:
there in a lineup of boys
were my father and his kid brother
the recognition and the shock:
a message finally delivered
to me from that place across time.

David Tanklefsky

BELOW THE STATION

From below the station
Where the commuter rail grinds
Southward from here
To Boston,
A breaking of levers and congruent ground,
Pebbles and bigger things.

In 6th grade we put pennies on the tracks
Me and neil and phil and bobby.
Neil moved to texas,
The rest of us are here.
"It'll knock it right off its fucking rails,"
But it just flattened our pennies.

And when it blew past
I though about lying below it
In between the tracks
And I was sure if I lay really still
That train would run right past me.

David Tanklefsky

YOUR EYES WILL WILT LIKE DAFFODILS

Your eyes will wilt like daffodils
Or water flooding crescent hills
But some sing sadder songs than these
That buckle old, ill-tempered knees.
There's beauty in your Saturdays
   Your sadder days
     Your youthful and
       Your ladder days
And this is true in all you do
  A trip to the market
   Or Waterloo
     Or feeding canaries at the Stonehill Zoo.
And time makes wrinkles were you lay
  By dark green sheets lurk
   Shadows of grey
    And withered things you'll never say
While time brings splinters and winter's chill
  Like water flooding crescent hills
  And eyes that wilt
   Like daffodils.

David Tanklefsky

ON TURNING ONE HUNDRED AND ONE

IN THE PARK

She was wrapped.
Sheathed in corduroy,
Pressed against the intimacy of every labor
Of one century and one one hundredth of the next.
Her dining partner, the youngun, not a day over
eighty-five.
"We're celebration her 101st birthday."
I can't recall her saying much of anything
The corners of her weighty lips struggled to form a
cracked, caked smile.
She sat below a glistening sky, as if aware of the
occasion,
The 36,865th of 36,865 days.
I wanted to tell her that she was a triumph,
That she was victorious in every verse,
That today was tomorrow and tomorrow today
And yesterday something she could remember or
forget
And that she was still the human spirit, breathing and
being,
To be one hundred and one dining in the park.
But all my meekest voices could muster was
"Happy Birthday."

David Donavel

CLEARING

After the storm the light was clean
and dry as fresh linen.
The August corn stood cool along the fences
tossed by a golden wind
and sidewalks were scrubbed
like seaside stones.
If this is the light that scours
summer from the year,
what is my heart's quickening?
And how do marigolds light
the scattered patches in the yard?

Even though the green-gold grasses dry
and snap beneath my feet,
I am joyful in my walking.
Yesterday swarming swallows
clustered on the roadside wires;
the willow wept its slender leaves
like tears along the wind.

Maples lose their leaves like
all my yellow summer hours;
flowers nod in the cleansing light.
In the deep sky the last feathered clouds
whisper, whisper,
"Now."

Emily Weston

AFTERNOON STORM

The rain on the island came down hard on the tin roof that day. But soon that got to be too much for the roof to handle, so the water all rushed down into the living room. We didn't have any buckets, so we let the rain roll down the red brick walls and onto the red brick floor. It wasn't a proper house anyway. My bedroom was off to the side of the living room, and when I opened my door in the morning, I could see the water cascading down like a waterfall. I'd never seen a real one before.

My family had lived here since I was two. It was a cheap set of cabinas, and we lived in the cheapest of the lot because my mother believed the best should be for the tourists. The cabinas were all pretty grungy though, and the people who stayed in them were pretty grungy too, so it didn't make much difference. Once my mom caught me outside the shower room spying on a woman who had a large purple butterfly tattooed on her lower back, and I wasn't let out of the house for a week.

The people cursed a lot. I could hear then through the walls. I decided to curse in front of my mom once because I dropped a bunch of grapes on the floor and she didn't let me out of the house for two weeks. But my friends who lived in town ten minutes down the beach would come and whisper through the air conditioner while I told them about the purple butterfly and the curse words. They went home and cursed in front of their parents. I was twelve. It was good on the island.

Usually, the rain comes down in five-minute bursts, but maybe because it was the beginning of the rainy season, the rain decided not to stop for the rest of that week. We were all full up because the mainlanders had heard that it wasn't raining in the off-season Caribbean and they all rushed down for the weather. They were real mad when it rained.

On the first day, one woman was crying on the phone because she and her husband had gotten married on the spur of the moment because the nice weather down here in the off season would have made a real nice cheap honeymoon. The husband just sat under the balcony of an upstairs cabina reading *USA Today* and smoking a cigar and watching the rain from behind his sunglasses. I didn't like him.

My two friends, George and Ozzie, came over that afternoon. We were friends because we all knew how to swim and we all knew how to curse. None of us had been born on the island. No one born on the island could swim. They were all scared of the water.

We stripped down to our shorts and ran to the beach. It felt a lot later than four, even though we could still see the sun through the clouds. You can never escape the island sun except during a real hurricane. This wasn't a hurricane, though.

The rain was cold on our skin so we only hesitated for a second before jumping into the warm water. The first few steps into the ocean drag you down like you're in a dream and can't run. But the swimming is fine. We swam out a bit and treaded water. I said that I thought this woman staying at the cabins was nice. They asked about her breasts, and I said that wasn't important, and they laughed and talked about the local girls. They were all pretty but had mean fathers who didn't let them out. Even if they could go out you couldn't talk to them. Ozzie said that they stuck together in gangs so we couldn't really have anything to do with them even if we wanted to. But George said we would only have to wait a bit longer; at least, that's what people told him.

We had a contest to see who could dive down and bring up something from the bottom. We all brought up a handful of sand so nobody really won. When you go underwater and it's raining on the surface, you can hear it like you can hear the rain tapping on the tin roof except softer. I liked it underwater.

When I came back up, I could see my mother on the shore waving. She didn't like it when we swam out so far. The clouds were really coming in towards the island. It got very dark and felt even later. None of us wanted to be the first to suggest swimming back, so we stayed out there, treading water and talking about the best gas stations to buy cigarettes. We didn't smoke, but we might have liked to if any of the gas station men believed we were old enough. We pretended not to see my mother. No one could penetrate us. We could talk about girls and cigarettes and no one could give a damn.

The wind started to pick up, and we had to keep our eyes fixed on the shore to stay in front of the cabinas. The husband with the sunglasses was watching us. My mother had gone inside.

The cold rain kept coming down harder, but it felt good out there in the warm water. It was hard to see the shoreline now and the water had turned gray.

Ozzie was talking about how he tried to steal beer from a gas station once, but George and I didn't believe him, and then suddenly he started to yell. I didn't know what he was yelling about. He tried to start swimming towards the shore but went in the wrong direction. George took one look at Ozzie thrashing around and started in the right direction. He didn't look back. I went after Ozzie.

The lightning started, and when I looked up at the sky to see the bolts across the horizon, I thought about the waterfall outside my door with the rain and the light from the storm coming in through the mosquito screen. I couldn't decide whether I wanted to be back there or not.

I caught up with Ozzie. He hadn't gone too far. I grabbed his hair and yelled at him about what he was doing. The son of a bitch thought he was being attacked and tried to punch me in the head. He was a lousy shot and missed. People get this way sometimes when it's dark and the water turns gray.

He was cursing like hell, words that even the woman with the purple butterfly hadn't said, and he was pulling me down so I punched him in the face. I got him real good too, and then grabbed him around the chest to pull him in the right direction. What a son of a bitch.

I kept hold of him, and he became less panicked. It was difficult to pull him towards shore. He was shorter than me, but he seemed a lot heavier, especially now. His mouth was bleeding a lot where I'd hit him and that wasn't good. I didn't want blood in the water but it was already there. I didn't even know if we were going in the right direction anymore. My head hurt from the swimming and I hoped I wasn't bleeding.

I wanted to stop swimming, so I did for a bit and lay on my back with the salt of the water helping me keep hold of Ozzie. The ocean was still rough but he was calm. The rain coming down on my chest hurt a bit and it sort of reminded me of the woman crying on the phone. She had looked like a waterfall with her brown hair falling down over her face so from the side all you could see was the phone cord coming out of her hair. She wasn't really crying for the rain, though. Her eyes were too red for the rain, which isn't such a bad thing, but people just make it so when they're upset already.

I felt calmer and started kicking again and dragged Ozzie the way the people in school had taught those of us who could swim. What a son of a bitch. I thought about what some of the girls on the island would look like with a big purple butterfly on their lower back. That would be nice to see.

I thought I heard voices, which seemed to dim as I got closer because all I could hear was the rough water lapping against my head. Then my back scraped up against the stones of the beach and all the voices got suddenly louder. My mother was crying and grabbed me and Ozzie into her arms, stunned by the blood which wasn't even flowing very much. George was looking at us and said something about a shark and not knowing what was going on. Then he ran off. Son of a bitch. I pushed my mother away and tried to stand up by myself. It was hard, but I managed. The man with the sunglasses was standing with his wife watching us. I stood up for her and gave a nod to the man. I turned back and looked at the ocean.

It was really gray, and you couldn't see the sun anymore, but I guessed it was only five or something. I didn't know it could get like that so fast. Ozzie was sniffling a bit and before my father took him to get his lip fixed in the office, he turned around and gave me a dirty look. My mother took me into the house. She paused for a moment to look at the water pouring down in front of my bedroom door. We were both soaked, so it didn't matter if we went through it or not, and we did. I told her to leave me alone, so she handed me a towel and some blankets and told me to go bed. I was glad to feel something solid beneath me. She was mad and crying, and I did not want to look at her.

She didn't let me outside the house for a week, and during that time George came by and told me through the air conditioner that everyone in town knew what had happened. It was going round that I killed a shark. I liked that. When I was let out, I bought a shark tooth on a leather string at some junky old tourist shop and didn't say *no* when people asked me if it came from the shark I killed. George would go round saying I skinned it myself and gave him the hide. Ozzie came over that day too but didn't mention the tooth. He said "thanks" and we looked at the ground and mumbled "it's okay" for a bit and then went to see if there were any women in the shower room, but it didn't seem like that mattered much anymore.

The crying woman and the man had left the day before I was let out of the house, the day the rain stopped. I didn't get to see her again. I had tried to listen to them, but they weren't very loud so I think she stopped crying. The rain does that to people when they're on the island. I fell asleep the next couple of days remembering the waterfall, fingering the shark tooth. I think that was the first time I remember really being in love, though I don't know exactly with what.

Matthew Hill

EDEN

In high school we were too much in love, too entranced by each other's faces, the darting, quivering greenness of the outer pupils, the touch of each other's skin, the images of our bodies, to notice; of course, it had already taken root somewhere in our consciousness that something wasn't right, that we weren't meant for each other, that we wouldn't get married as our dreamy countenances and our entwined fingers seemed to imply. Most everything was in some form obscured: in youth we were always surrounded by beauty and emotion and impulse, those things which tend to pull yellow curtains over gray truths. Kathy and I found ourselves in these beautiful places often by mistake, but just as often by choice, and when it was by choice it was because we wanted these things to be obscured: we loved the bright yellow, hated the dark gray.

Like one day when we picked apples. We had slipped quietly out of last block and into my green Pontiac, heard the engine roar over the mist-covered parking lot, felt the wheels spin for a second before catching, and propelling us down the dirt road at the school exit. Kathy always had her hand on the radio, turning the spin-dial like it were a doorknob, but as if the door were locked: she never found what she liked, always listening for a second or two before twisting at it again. I drove fast—a crime that I admitted to (or bragged about), and that Kathy's mother despised—but it got us places fast, especially when we wanted to.

The farm was in the town next to ours, at the end of a twisting road without a yellow dividing line in the middle of it, a road that meandered through endless fields of corn and other crops— and it always seemed as if it were getting thinner the farther you drove, two lanes into one and a half, then to one; by the time you reached the farm, perched on a little hillside looking out over the valley, you had to put the windows up or the leaves from the cornstalks on the side of the road would come through and hit you in the chest. On that day that we picked apples Kathy kept leaning against me while I was driving, as if we were always taking right turns; I felt the ball of her shoulder against my bicep, the curved plane of her face on my shoulder. She had murmured, when the road narrowed to about one point three, whether we were there yet, in a childish voice—she knew I loved when she talked like that—and I had said only a few minutes more, and our points of impact had pushed harder on each other.

A bag was six dollars. The woman at the counter, late in her fifties, her hair wrapped up like swirled soft-serve ice cream, handed the bag to Kathy.

"You can fit about a dozen in there," she said. "Or a baker's, if you layer 'em right." She winked at us both, as if she knew we would try to stuff the bag full as possible, perhaps even submerge a few into our pockets, as if we were trying to be clever sinners but she knew what we were up to. "Don't go out past the fence," she added as we were heading through the squeaky swinging door. "Those apples ain't ripe yet." She tapped the counter lightly with her fingers, pasty and wide-knuckled, and smiled. She held the pose as we turned and headed outside. I remember wondering what she did when customers weren't there for her to help, but soon I abandoned the thought.

When you were a kid it was so easy to get lost in the endless rows of trees, spread in lines like an army across the rolling hills. My mother used to have a fit every time she couldn't find me: I would watch her from my nearby hiding spot, crouched down with my sneakers arched over the fallen, bruised apples, writhing presumably with little worms that to a child seemed like snakes; my mother would walk faster, would call louder, would eventually break into a run. But she never weaved in and out of trees, only ran back and forth down the one row. Eventually I would feel guilty about it, I think, or something like that, and I would come out. She never punished me for it. I would always say that I got lost. That I couldn't help it.

Kathy held onto my sleeve tightly, leading me through the branches left, then right, straight for two trees, then left again.

"What do you want us to do?" I said. "Get lost?"

"Exactly," she said, offering a devilish smile. "So lost that we'll never find a way out." Quickly she pulled right, straining the fabric of my shirtsleeve before I compensated and veered with her. She darted into the middle of two pines, whose branches were crossed like folded hands, and we broke through them recklessly, the needles scraping against our sides. Our breathing evolved from drawled gusts to spurts of contained laughter as we zigzagged across the apple orchard, left, right, left, right...

Of course, when you're trying to get lost you never really do. You pretend it for a minute, let yourself succumb to your imagination that you're unaware of how you got there. That the sun is directly above you, that there are no shadows, no trace of the path you left behind. You pretend that the past never existed, that all there is is the here-and-now, the short-order happiness, the whirlwind emotions. Kathy grappled around a sparse tree that appeared like a skeleton and halted before a wooden fence, rotting and brown, leaning sideways haphazardly and stretching and meandering across the hilly fields. Beyond it lay a minefield of verdant growth, the trees spread far apart amid patches of arch-like strands of grass, bent over and pointing down towards the earth.

"I'm going over it," Kathy said defiantly, pointing a finger at the fence, and clasping her other hand around my shoulder as if to say farewell.

"You wouldn't dare." I lowered my eyes to hers, attempting a note of austerity. "No one's allowed out there."

It was here that perfection was achieved, a line of sparkling beads floating invisibly between us, ends tied at our eyes. It was here that there were no mistakes, where the world around us was insignificant, irrelevant, redundant: where its only purpose was to bring us together in harmony, to clasp our hands together and impel us to dance to imaginary harps.

Kathy lifted a well-concealed apple from her jacket pocket and held it in her left hand, groping it between her fingers, her hand outstretched between us.

"It's forbidden to steal, too," she said, raising her eyebrow slightly, twinkling her eyes perfectly, as if she could control their loveliness. She moved almost unnoticeably closer, her torso inches from mine, and lifted the apple to her opened lips, sinking her pearl teeth into the red fruit—the familiar click of the skin breaking, the knife-on-paper splitting of the juicy substance beneath. I caught her hand as it reached up to my mouth, led it gently to the opening, and bit into it, letting the sweet juice slide down my throat. We were touching at the waist now, and my left hand had slipped unconsciously to her hip, pulling her closer, and the apple was between our lips, held lazily by her hand—but now it was falling; now just a part of the world, now only meant to bring us closer—and the ripe taste of the apple faded, was gently smothered by the touch of her lips.

"Well," she said, pulling away for an instant, "what else is forbidden?"

I smiled. "Nothing."

She lifted her finger to my lips, as if to quiet me, and turned furtively to the fence, pressing her palm against a leaning plank and lifting her leg over. Her foot touched the ground on the other side, the sideways fence rising up between her legs and barely touching her there, leaving a faded, dash-like stain of mud. She looked down at her pants with a humiliated grin, a pink color rising in her cheeks, and pressed her legs together tightly. I laughed as I approached the fence, sidestepping it with ease, and a cool wind rustled through the orchard.

On the other side of the fence she was waiting there, her legs pressed together and her hands held behind her back, presumably clenching the empty bag we had yet to fill. Her hair danced lightly on her shoulders as the wind continued, now coupled with a faint howl echoing in the trees, and the varied calls of birds as they lifted off from the swaying branches and into the swirling sky. She motioned with her hand towards the fields beyond, stretching before us, but I was telling her to let me see, to let me see, and I put my hands gently on her waist, eliciting a hushed giggle from her; she was attempting to get away now as my fingernails lightly tickled her sides; now she was turning, now running confusedly, now laughing and breathing wildly; now leaning, falling with the support of my arms. Now us falling together into a patch of grass, her on my side, still giggling.

"Let me see!"

She attempted crawling away, and the mud beneath us reached up and covered her knees and her hands; but her ankles were in my grasp, and before long she was back in my arms again, stains of earth marked sporadically over her clothes.

"Never," she said. "I'll never let you see..." And she fell into another kiss, lying on top of me, her hair falling on either side of my face, covering the light around us for an instant. I rolled over on my side, saturated by the joke, and put my hand around her leg and attempted a glimpse at the stain, but she clenched her legs around mine, the stain still concealed. She was kissing my neck now, seductively tracing her fingers along my chest.

"Let's get married," I whispered as she moved on top of me. She only laughed slightly. "We'll run away and live away in the country, like this."

"Like this? It might get lonely," she said, resting her head in the glove-like enclosure between my chest and my chin. "It would only be us two."

"Yeah. You want more than that?" I said, laughing. I slipped my fingertips under the frayed edge of her shirt, drumming them in succession, from pinky to pointer, on her back like a wave.

"I don't know."

A silence enveloped us as if the wind had lost interest.

"It'll be just you and me, Kath. No school, no moms whining about how fast I drive." She giggled quietly, almost out of politeness. "And we'll have an apple farm. An orchard like this. You can be the old woman standing at the counter, telling those kids not to break the rules."

She seemed quieted by the possibility.

"And we can have kids, too—kids who'll fall in love just like us, generations of lovers, skipping last block of school just to be together, apple pickers like us who'll get married and live together and have kids and start it all over again—"

As Kathy fell silent on top of me I felt the weight of her small frame; I became aware of her body expanding and tightening as she breathed; I felt the slight murmur, the constant pulse, of her heart faintly against my ribs—and then, the wet pin drop of a tear against my Adam's apple.

"Kath—?"

She looked up, tilting herself away from me. Her eyes were red-rimmed and swollen, and her cheeks had taken on an uncomfortable pinkish tone that sank my heart when I saw them. A few strands of hair fell in curved lines, sticking to her face, wet with tears. She was quivering slightly, resting on her left arm, locked erect and planted on the ground, and remained silent.

"Kath, what's the matter?"

The sinking feeling in my stomach gave way for something to rise—something I had hidden, perhaps, from my consciousness: something I hated, despised, which I longed to cover up with layers of happy memories and hopeful dreams. In her face I saw a similar reaction take place, and in an instant our eyes met; the string of beads, of perfection, seemed to be ripping and falling, the beads spilling over us in the form of tears, descending on our own bodies, on the crestfallen grass.

"We're lost," Kathy said finally, pulling back even more and resting on her knees. She had lifted her gaze above mine, looking out over the hills. "We're lost, we're lost…"

And we were. I raised my eyes to the countryside, spreading out before us like a tortuous maze; and the waning sunlight fell in uneven patches over the hills, submerging the little valleys in thick darkness and pouring down on us through hole-filled clouds. The path we had taken was impossible to discern amid the rows and lines of similar trees, the similar entwined branches, the same fallen apples. And as the clouds roamed aimlessly through the sky, a gray light descended around us, the yellow light of midday forgotten.

Ron Howland

A LITANY OF THINGS TO FEAR

Like too-old children snuggling their own warmth
in a wet bed, we snuggle our children down
into our solaces. We write notes
for the little inadequate engines
of their souls, for all the undone homework,
theirs and ours. Then when they embarrass us
we skitter the word *esteem* like a red
life saver over school linoleum
because somewhere down the line
the dream withered to a voice begging not to be
found. Just spared. We want to spare them.
We put our hands on the shoulders of our grown
children. We joke out explanations
for their acting not wholly unlike oafs,
decorating them in the third person
like a Christmas tree hogging the sofa.
We have won with bloodless tactics
a peace worse than any siege of fears,
worse than hunger, failure, loneliness
and the other things that qualify us
for rest or dignity or whatever
it was that was once supposed to matter.
Except love. Nothing *makes* love possible.
It is no more possible than stars,
than the ache that stretches beyond the skin
and is older than skin, no more possible
than a universe leaping into time
scented with berries and the quiverings
of light in the sky of a summer night
into which they will be born despite us.

Andre Dubus

LETTER TO A WRITERS' WORKSHOP

A writers' workshop has met in my home on Thursday nights since the fall of 1987. Writers come for a few months or years, then leave, and someone else comes. In June of 1992, Christopher Tilghman and Jim Thompson, who had been members of the workshop since its beginning, came to my house so we could talk about what we were doing on Thursday nights. We were not doing well; I was a poor leader. Afterward, I wrote this letter to the writers.

Chris and Jim and I talked about writing, and reading to people, and listening to what people say. We have twelve passionate writers and, quite naturally and quite morally, when we hear stories, we talk about them. I've felt for some time that we talk more than we should, because we only hear the stories, we do not read them, and cannot possibly, as a group, be accurate. It has taken me a long time to admit that I generally miss a page or two when I'm hearing a story. A good line or image sometime stimulates me so, absorbs me so, that I simply don't hear the next page. We've tried giving copies to everyone to read, and it's too much to ask or receive. We'd like to meet now, beginning the Thursday after Labor Day, for pleasure and encouragement. Chris said: "We're listening as writers; we should listen as readers."

So we'd like to have two readers a night, and limit discussions to fifteen minutes. That gives everyone time to say what, in general, is good about a story, and what needs work. This is a way of getting twelve people away from a writer's desk, of setting writers free to find editors they can trust. After I've read on Thursday nights, I've spent an inordinate amount of time—days, weeks, more—trying to reclaim my story or essay at my desk, get it back from all those voices I respect. Over the past year or more, those voices have been with me as I write, and I've had to concentrate more, to get rid of them. I've always thought of someone while writing, from time to time, testing a line on that person's eye (not ear): Chekhov, and wives and girlfriends. I'm sharing this with you because other writers in the group have shared the same experience with me. I like Chris's idea: call it a reading group, not a workshop. Perhaps workshops are better when they consist of ten or fewer rookies and one veteran whose job is to draw from the rookies whatever is there.

When I say we talk too much, I do not mean it in the usual sense. I mean there is too much light in the room, it dazzles, and most discussions last year left me drawn and quartered of spirit. I mean discussions of other people's work as well as my own. And what else can we expect when we read to eleven people whose vocation it is to write? We respond as writers, we rewrite stories by saying how they could be done differently, and very often we are talking about the way each of us would write the story, or a scene or passage in it. Even when we are right, there are too many of us. Certainly twelve people can disagree and all be right about how a story could be written. "The Short Happy Life of Francis Macomber" would not have survived us without a stubborn author. I mention that story because I can read it in two absolutely different ways: if I take the title as ironic, I like the story, for it shows the foolishness of these folk; if I take the title seriously, I don't like the story. I've talked to a lot of writers over the decades about this story, and confusion abounds. Thomas Williams, God bless him, said it best: "It's either one of Hemingway's best stories or one of his worst, depending on how you read it."

And, oh, what is important is that Hemingway wrote it and we can read it, and if he made mistakes, if he left things unclear, well, that's better than scurrying home to revise and revise and revise and make it clear for everyone. Because no one knows where the words are coming from anyway, no one writing sincerely (Nadine Gordimer defined *sincerity* in *My Son's Story* as "never speaking from an idea of oneself"); no one knows where the images and the very story are coming from. We sit at the desk and try to concentrate absolutely, and concentration takes us to the place where the words and images and stories are. This is not a place we can reach every time we want to; it is a strange place; and, very often, reading galleys of my work, I have found a sentence difficult to understand, as though someone else had written it; and, very often too, I have been surprised by feelings of a character, and the revelations in the character's spirit. This summer, I read *Peace Is Every Step* by Thich Nhat Hanh, a Buddhist monk, and as I read of what he calls "mindfulness," I realized why writing and physical exercise have been so deeply pleasurable for me despite or because of the effort they demand: while doing both of those, if I am concentrating, I am one with the man I normally am not and, achieving or receiving that, I am one with people and truths I will never know when I am my normal self again: driving a car, or watching men throw a baseball, or talking with friends.

And to achieve or receive these truths on the page, each of us has to proceed alone, in our own way, and very often that way is a clumsy one. At the Iowa Writers' Workshop, Richard Yates taught us *From Here to Eternity*, a novel he loved. Yates said to us: If Jones had been in a workshop here, I would have said: "You know Jim, your first chapter reads like the first chapter of a short book; but this is a very long book, so I think you ought to rewrite that first chapter'; and a year from now, I'd say, 'How's the revision of that first chapter going?' and he'd say, 'Oh swell, Dick, swell,' and he'd keep on writing his great book." Toby Wolff heard me read a story in Ohio, where we were working together for a few summer days, and afterward, over drinks, he said: "I think at the end you played the organ just a little too long." I not only knew precisely what he meant but I agreed, and I knew he would have written the end better, and as a reader I would have enjoyed it more; and I knew that I wouldn't change what I had written, because that was the only way I could write it, and if I changed it, it wouldn't be mine anymore. We can't make them perfectly, only as best as we can. Hemingway once said that he had very little natural talent and what people called his style was simply his effort to overcome his lack of talent. Don't take that lightly. What is art if not a concentrated and impassioned effort to make something with the little we have, the little we see?

We shall remain flexible. This is a talented and generous group, and everyone will be served. Some I've spoken to feel the need, at times, for more extensive criticism; they will give us manuscripts to take home and read; then we can meet to discuss the story, rather than listen to it. One writer I've spoken to feels more free this summer, "writing alone," and would like to choose someone else's story to read to us. I'd love to read Chekhov's "A Woman's Kingdom," which I read again this summer; it is one of the most magnificent stories I've ever read, but it's forty-seven pages long in a Modern Library edition, so probably eighty in manuscript, and would take too long.

People who want to read work in progress must be extremely stubborn; a little hearing impairment would be helpful. We've been at least potentially lethal in the past, and I'm impressed by Edie Clark's tenacity: finishing her book after those long discussions of its sections. I don't believe I would have been able to.

If Hemingway in his thirties were among us, would there really be any more to say after he read than: "Ernest, this is beautiful writing, you took me to Africa, Francis and Margot and Wilson are real, it's an exciting story, but Ernest: Am I supposed to feel that Francis is a foolish boy in a man's body doing foolish things in Africa? Or do you want me to believe Francis actually had a breakthrough?" Or, as a young female student of mine years ago said: "He had to end that story with Francis getting killed because, believe me, when they got back to New York it was going to be the same old stuff again, she was going to cheat on him again, and he'd be a wimp again..."

And so it goes. Beautiful, isn't it? "It's what they call flesh we're in. And a fine old dance it is" (Christopher Fry wrote that), and we're not going to understand it all in one Thursday evening in Haverhill, Massachusetts, so let's listen to stories and be honest but try to stay general rather than specific and let the mysteries go home with the writer.